With the abrupt closure of t
merce International in July
learned of the largest fraud
Kochan and Bob Whittingto
which purported to offer M
haven for terror gangs, arms dealers, drugs money launderers, international security services and sleazy dictators.

Drawing on unique sources inside the banking and security establishments, the authors show how Pakistani financier Agha Hasan Abedi and a clique of Pakistani financiers charmed and swindled oil-rich sheikhs, how leading world politicians were inveigled into corrupt schemes through lavish spending on charities and entertainment; and how BCCI used billions of dollars of depositors' money to make loans to its Middle East shareholders for secret nominee purchases of US banks.

Kochan and Whittington also examine in detail crucial unanswered questions: why the Central Intelligence Agency did not act when it learnt about corruption in the mid eighties, why accountants Price Waterhouse signed off its books for so many years; and why the Bank of England failed to follow up evidence of fraud and deceit. And with hundreds of thousands of small investors left stranded by the collapse, the authors ask: after BCCI who can trust their own bank?

*Bankrupt* is a lucid, fast-paced account of the financial scandal of all time.

X

## About the Authors

Nick Kochan has written extensively about fraud and banking. The co-author of *The Guinness Affair*, he formerly worked at the *Sunday Times* as an investigative journalist. Now a freelance, Kochan writes for the *Sunday Telegraph*, the *Independent on Sunday*, and *Euromoney*.

Bob Whittington is a former business affairs producer for Independent Television News and now a full-time author and business journalist. He is the author of *Kill for a Client*, charting the rise and fall of Bain and Co., the management consultant company.

# Bankrupt:

## THE BCCI FRAUD

NICK KOCHAN
and
BOB WHITTINGTON

LONDON
VICTOR GOLLANCZ LTD
1991

To
LRL, artist and friend extraordinaire,
and
Fiona Whittington, without whose patience . . .

First published in Great Britain 1991
by Victor Gollancz Ltd
14 Henrietta Street, London WC2E 8QJ



A CIP record for this book is available
from the British Library

ISBN 0 575 05279 1

Typeset in Great Britain by
Rowland Phototypesetting Ltd,
Bury St Edmunds, Suffolk
and printed and bound in Great Britain by
Cox and Wyman Ltd, Reading, Berks.

# Contents

# Acknowledgements

Many people have contributed to this account of the BCCI story. First, there are the many actors in the saga who were kind enough to spare us their time, without expecting any recognition. Then there are those who have assisted the authors with their time and skills. Among these is Benedict Milne who contributed extensively to Chapter 7 and prepared the index, Loli Cardenoso who translated *The Kings of the Money Launderers* by Daniel Gonzalez from the Spanish, Laura Lehman who developed a chronology, Anna Kochan who translated from the French and the late great Max Kantor who gathered research in the United States.

Many Asian depositors have also given generously of their time. The antics of the Muslim bank have done nothing but harm for the wider and honourable Asian business community.

Nick Kochan
Bob Whittington
London, November 1991

# Cast of Characters

## Protagonists

**Agha Hasan Abedi** Founder and president, BCCI. A mystic with spell-binding oratory. A brilliant marketing man, say his friends, never a banker. Commanded fanatical loyalty and used a formidable contacts book to build his dream of the biggest Muslim bank in the world. Suffered two heart attacks in 1988. Resigned 4 October 1990.

**Swaleh Naqvi** Chief executive and financial brains of BCCI. Resigned with Abedi.

## Principals

**Kamal Adham** Former head of Saudi Intelligence, major investor in BCCI and First American. Half-brother of Iffat, wife of late King Faisal. Shareholder in Capcom Financial Services.

**Syed Ziauddin Ali Akbar** Head of BCCI treasury, founder of Capcom. Jailed on drugs charges 1989, released. Arrested in 1991 in Calais on drugs laundering charges.

**Amjad Awan** Manager of BCCI in Panama, handled Noriega's personal account. Jailed for twelve years for involvement in Tampa drugs money laundering.

**Faisal Saud al-Fulaij** Chairman of Kuwait Airways from 1964 to 1977, also chairman of Kuwait International Finance Company, a BCCI affiliate. Alleged to have received an unsecured loan of $3.5 million to buy stock in First American.

**Zafar Iqbal** Manager of BCCI subsidiary in Abu

Dhabi, made acting CEO on resignation of Naqvi in 1990.

**El-Sayed Jawhary** Saudi investor and nominee in First American, shareholder in Capcom Financial Services.

**Hassan Kazmi** Secretary, ICIC Foundation.

**Abdul Raouf Khalil** Saudi businessman, invested in Financial General.

**Ghanim al-Mazrui** Head of Sheikh Zayed's private department, succeeding Dharwaish in 1981. Also secretary-general of Abu Dhabi Investment Authority which owned 10 per cent of BCCI Holdings. On board of directors BCCI (Luxembourg).

**Ghaith Pharaon** Saudi financier, shareholder and nominee. Owner of loss-making Attock Oil Company. Bought National Bank of Georgia from Bert Lance and others. Also bought Independence Bank in Encino, California. Alleged front man for BCCI. Formerly on board of Harvard Business School.

**Masihur Rahman** Chief financial officer, BCCI.

**Sheikh Zayed bin-Sultan al-Nahyan** Ruler of Abu Dhabi, family and state own 77 per cent of BCCI.

## Players

**Velayat Hussein Abedi** Ex-United Bank, close to Naqvi, later head of London operations.

**Imtiaz Ahmed** Head of credit division, BCCI.

**Robert Altman** Lawyer and partner of Clark Clifford. Helped defence of BCCI officers in Tampa drugs trial. President of First American, married to Lynda Carter, American TV's Wonder Woman.

**Asif Baakza** Manager BCCI corporate unit, arrested

on drugs money laundering charges.

**Akbar Bilgrami** BCCI manager Latin America, arrested in Tampa drugs sting.

**Jack Blum** Washington lawyer and former congressional investigator. Helped uncover the Tampa drugs money laundering ring. Took his suspicions about BCCI to Robert Morgenthau when faced with what he took to be stonewalling from the Justice Department.

**Nazir Chinoy** Former manager BCCI Paris, arrested in 1988 on drugs money laundering charges.

**Basheer Chowdry** Head of BCCI's UK division.

**Clark Clifford** Senior partner of Clifford and Warnke, lawyers. Doyen of the Washington legal circuit, friend of presidents. Guided investors in First American Bancshares takeover. Chairman of First American in 1980. Resigned after storm broke.

**Abdullah Dharwaish** Former head of Sheikh Zayed's private department until 1981. Investor in Financial General.

**Khuaro Elley** BCCI executive.

**Mustafa Gokal** Eldest of three brothers, ran Gulf Shipping group which became principal bad debtor of BCCI.

**Abbas Gokal** Driving force of Gokal family.

**Daniel Gonzalez** Deputy manager, BCCI Panama, author of *The Kings of the Money Launderers*.

**Moizul Haque** UK regional manager, handled affairs of Control Securities Nazmu Virani.

**Sheikh Khalifa bin-Zayed al-Nahyan** Crown prince of Abu Dhabi.

**Khalid bin-Mahfouz** Son of Salim bin-Mahfouz, founder of Saudi Arabia's National Commercial Bank, on board of directors BCCI (Luxembourg). Family had

20 per cent stake in BCCI and at one stage considered buying bank, then sold out.

**Robert Morgenthau** New York District Attorney. Launched his own secret investigation into BCCI after tip-off from Blum in 1989. Brought first indictments in BCCI case.

**Samir Najmeddin** Financial adviser to Abu Nidal.

**General Manuel Noriega** Former Panamanian dictator in pay of CIA. Toppled in US invasion in 1989. On trial for drugs smuggling. Also faces series of indictments along with BCCI for taking billions of dollars out of the country's economy. Alleged to have made full use of BCCI bank accounts around the world to launder money.

**M. R. Pirbhai** Friend of Abedi, legal consultant.

**Ghassan Qassem** BCCI manager London, worked with MI5.

**William von Raab** Former US Commissioner of Customs.

**Iqbal Rizvi** High-flyer in charge of Europe, Africa and South America.

**Saigols** Wealthy textile family, Pakistan.

**Abdul Sami** Abedi favourite, number two in bank until resignation.

**Saleem Sidiqi** Ex-United Bank, head of BCCI inspection department.

**Ameer Siddiki** Head of BCCI credit committee.

## Supporting Cast

**Rabia Abedi** Abedi's second wife, former air hostess.

**Abu Nidal** International terrorist.

**Aijaz Afridi** Vice-President, First American.

**Mohammed Azmatullah** Close to Naqvi, helped manage 'Naqvi files'.

**Zulfiqar Ali Bhutto** Former Prime Minister of Pakistan.

**Munther Bilbeisi** Jordanian arms dealer caught smuggling coffee.

**Lord Justice Bingham** Leading Bingham inquiry, UK.

**Sir Nicholas Browne-Wilkinson** Vice-Chancellor High Court, UK.

**Roy Carlson** Ex-Bank of America, head of National Bank of Georgia.

**Jimmy Carter** Former US President, friend of Abedi who contributed to Carter's charitable Global 2000 programme.

**Azizullah Choudry** BCCI credit department.

**Leonel Figueroa** Former President of Central Reserve Bank, Peru.

**Alan Garcia** President of Peru between 1985 and 1990. Accused of placing hundreds of millions of Central Bank reserves currency with BCCI to avoid country's creditors.

**Robert Gates** Deputy Director of CIA.

**Mohammed Hafiz** BCCI company secretary.

**Sheikh Hamad bin-Mohammed al-Sharqi** Ruler of Emirate of Fujairah.

**John Heimann** Former head of the US office of the comptroller of the currency.

**Eugene Hollis** Georgia senator who introduced Abedi to Bert Lance.

**Sheikh Humaid bin-Rashid al-Naomi** Ruler of Emirate of Ajman.

**Pierre Jaans** Director-General of Luxembourg Monetary Institute. In 1984 he first called for college of regulators to supervise BCCI more closely.

**El-Sayed Jawhary** Kamal Adham's assistant.

**John Kerry** Democratic Party senator from Massachusetts. Chairman of Senate Foreign Relations Sub-committee on Terrorism, Narcotics and International Communications. Scourge of BCCI with hearing into scandal through the Senate Banking Committee.

**Ayub Khan** Former Prime Minister of Pakistan.

**General Yahya Khan** Former Prime Minister of Pakistan.

**Leonard Kingshott** CEO of planned restructured bank.

**Bert Lance** Georgia banker, former budget director to President Carter, until forced to resign for alleged banking practices. Advised group of Arab investors trying to take over Financial General Bancshares, Washington DC. Sold his National Bank of Georgia shares to Pharaon.

**Robin Leigh-Pemberton** Governor of the Bank of England.

**Donald Macleod** Financial director, Western Isles Council, UK.

**Bob Magness** Founder Tele-Communications Inc., USA, and shareholder in Capcom Financial Services.

**Charles Mathias, Jr** Former Republican senator (Maryland). One of two outside directors on six man board of First American Bancshares. Replaced late Stuart Symington, senator from Missouri.

**Carlos Menem** President of Argentina. Former in-laws implicated in money laundering. Accused of favouritism towards Pharaon.

**Eugene Metzger** Washington lawyer, disgruntled National Bank of Georgia shareholder.

**William Middendorf** Chairman of Financial General,

also keen to sell stake in National Bank of Georgia.

**Christopher Morris** Partner of Touche Ross, the liquidators.

**Hector Neyra** General manager, Central Reserve Bank, Peru.

**David Paul** Chairman of CenTrust Savings and Loan, one of the biggest S and L failures. Ghaith Pharaon was one of the largest outside shareholders in CenTrust.

**Price Waterhouse** BCCI auditors.

**Achai and Sushma Puri** Directors of Capcom Financial Services.

**Sheikh Quabus** Sultan of Oman.

**Nadir Rahim** Head of human resources, special responsibility for India.

**Sheikh Rashid** Ruler of Dubai.

**Dildar Rezvi** In charge of hospitality, BCCI.

**Larry Romrell** Vice-President, Tele-Communications Inc., and shareholder in Capcom Financial Services.

**Dr Ali Reza Saheb** Abedi's early Iranian contact.

**Abdur Sakhia** Munther Bilbeisi's BCCI contact.

**Ali Mohammed Shorafa** Nominee, invested in Financial General.

**Brian Smouha** Partner in Touche Ross.

**Charles B. Stauffacher** Second outside director of First American.

**Touche Ross** Provisional liquidators of BCCI.

**Keith Vaz MP** Depositors' campaign leader.

**General Zia al-Haq** Former President of Pakistan.

# Chronology of Events

**1922** •Agha Hasan Abedi born a Shi'ite Muslim in Lucknow, India, the son of administrator for the Rajah of Mahmoodabad.

**1960** •Abedi founds United Bank Ltd with Rupees 10 million injection of cash from the Saigols.

**1972** •*September:* Abedi and a group of investors found BCCI with $2.5 million capital, and the intention to provide commercial banking services in the Middle East and the UK.

**1973** •BCCI opens Green Park branch in London.
•BCCI incorporates in the Cayman.

**1978** •*January 4:* Ghaith Pharaon buys National Bank of Georgia.
•Bank of America cuts its stake in BCCI back 40 per cent to 24 per cent and declines to take part in new rights issue.
•*July/August:* Netherlands Antilles-based Credit and Commerce American Holdings and Credit and Commerce American Investment are formed.

**1979** •Ernst and Whinney (now Ernst and Young) first voice concern about there being two sets of auditors for the bank.

**1980** •The first Third World Prize of $100,000 is awarded by Third World Foundation, a new charitable organisation started by BCCI and run by Altaf Gauhar.

**1981** •*August:* CCAH takes over Financial General.

•*September:* Abedi founds the BCCI Foundation.
•Amjad Awan takes over manager's job in Panama and builds up links with Noriega.
•Samir Najmeddin opens Abu Nidal-based account in Park Lane with $48 million deposit.

**1982** •*January 19:* Noriega becomes a client of BCCI's Panama branch.
•SZA Akbar becomes head of BCCI's treasury operation.
•*August:* Financial General changes its name to First American Bancshares.

**1983** •BCCI buys a Colombian bank with branches in Medellin and Cali, centres for the cocaine trade.

**1984** •Pierre Jaans, Director-General of the Luxembourg Monetary Institute, makes first attempt to establish college of regulators.

**1984** •*June:* Capcom Financial Services founded.

**1985** •*January:* BCCI acquires the National Bank of Georgia.
•Luxembourg Monetary Institute asks Price Waterhouse to launch an inquiry into BCCI.

**1986** •*January 20:* Price Waterhouse tells Rahman it has found fraud in the treasury.
•*June:* $430 million losses are discovered in the BCCI treasury. The college of regulators is established.
•*July 29:* BCCI brings in the bin-Mahfouz family as investors.
•*September 30:* The CIA is said to have circu-

lated a report on BCCI to law enforcement agencies. 'In 1986 the CIA knew BCCI was a criminal enterprise and owned the First American Bank of Washington and they told a number of government agencies,' said Senator John Kerry later.

- CIA uses BCCI for intelligence operations in Afghanistan and in secret arms sales from the US to Iran in 1986, aided by Adnam Khashoggi.
- *December 2:* Operation C-Chase sting begins.

**1987**
- *April:* Move to appoint single auditor.
- *Autumn:* British intelligence allegedly learns of BCCI's connections with Abu Nidal.
- *December:* college of regulators is created.

**1988**
- *February:* Abedi has two heart attacks.
- *October 11:* US Federal prosecutor in Tampa charges BCCI Holdings SA of Luxembourg, its two principal subsidiaries and eight employees with 'conspiring to possess with intent to distribute' cocaine.

**1989**
- *October 2:* bin-Mahfouz family sell their stake in BCCI Group.

**1990**
- *January:* Price Waterhouse finds big holes in loan book left by massive unrepaid loans.
- *January 16:* BCCI staff plead guilty to laundering charges in Tampa.
- *February 5:* BCCI is fined $15.3 million for drugs laundering offence. Five former BCCI executives are jailed for up to twelve years.
- *March:* Price Waterhouse tells BCCI it may

have uncovered transactions that 'may have been either false or deceitful'.

- *April:* Naqvi flies to Abu Dhabi in search of more funds.
- *April–May:* BCCI announces losses of $498 million for 1989 and plans for a radical restructuring. Abu Dhabi government takes control with 77 per cent of the shares. BCCI's centre of operation moves to Abu Dhabi.
- *July 28:* Naqvi files to Abu Dhabi.
- *October 4:* Abedi and Naqvi are forced to resign at board meeting.

**1991**

- *January 4:* Federal Reserve formally investigates the ownership of First American.
- *March 4:* The Bank of England appoints Price Waterhouse to carry out investigation under 41 (1) of Banking Act.
- *June 22:* Price Waterhouse investigation is delivered to the Bank of England. This provides 'the first and overwhelming evidence of a fraudulent nature'.
- *July:* Senate Banking Committee announces full-scale investigation into BCCI.
- *July 2:* After day-long meeting the Bank of England supervisors take the decision to close BCCI.
- *July 3:* Luxembourg puts the Gokal family's Gulf International Holdings SA into administration.
- *July 5:* The Bank of England announces the closure of BCCI at 1 p.m.
- *July 10:* Western Isles Council reveals losses of £20 million.

- *July 19:* UK Chancellor Norman Lamont announces inquiry to be headed by Lord Justice Bingham.
- *July 29:* Robert Morgenthau, New York DA, publishes eighteen-page indictment. Federal Reserve begins enforcement proceedings and announces $200 million fine on BCCI.
- *July 30:* UK High Court gives bank four months' reprieve before winding-up.
- *August 1:* US Senate committee on Terrorism and Narcotics opens its proceedings into BCCI.
- *August 8:* Masihur Rahman appears before Senate sub-committee.
- *August 13:* Clifford and Altman resign from the board of First American. Nicholas Katzenbach, former US Attorney General, takes over.
- *September 8:* The Abu Dhabi government arrests thirty BCCI executives, including Naqvi and Iqbal.
- *December 2:* The date is set for winding-up order in the UK.

# Abbreviations used in the Text

| | |
|---|---|
| **BCC(E)** | Bank of Credit and Commerce (Emirates) |
| **BCCI** | Bank of Credit and Commerce International |
| **BCP** | Banque de Commerce et Placements |
| **BNP** | Banque Nationale de Paris |
| **BoA** | Bank of America |
| **CCAH** | Credit and Commerce American Holdings |
| **FABNY** | First American Bank of New York |
| **FGB** | Financial General Bancshares |
| **ICIC** | International Credit and Investment Company |
| **LACRO** | Latin American and Caribbean Office (BCCI) |
| **NBG** | National Bank of Georgia |
| **SNCB** | National Commercial Bank of Saudi Arabia |
| **UBS** | Union Bank of Switzerland |
| **C-Chase** | Calibre-Chase |
| **Operation Q** | Operation Qassem |
| **SFO** | Serious Fraud Office (UK) |

# Introduction

'This indictment spells out the largest bank fraud in world history. BCCI was operated as a corrupt and criminal organisation throughout its entire nineteen-year history. It systematically falsified its records. It knowingly allowed itself to be used to launder the illegal income of drug sellers and other criminals. And it paid bribes and kickbacks to public officials.' – Robert Morgenthau, New York District Attorney, 29 July 1991.

The Bank of Credit and Commerce International masterminded the most lurid bank fraud yet uncovered and also by far the biggest. Pakistani conmen and newly enriched Arab sheikhs, terrorists and secret services, arms financiers and politicians conspired together under the same roof. Everyone manipulated the bank for his own ends and some made millions. The price for this orgy of abuse is estimated at $10 billion, and the figure is rising. There has also been a human toll. Thousands of employees have been thrown out of work, and depositors have been left penniless.

Since 1972, when the bank was founded, BCCI gathered round it a dubious and shady clientele for whom the bank provided much more than traditional banking. But although there was solid evidence of wrongdoing, including drugs money laundering and arms financing, regulators and law enforcement waited a decade to bring the bent bank to book. When the bank was closed, there was a host of excuses. The bank regulators claimed lack of proof of wrongdoing, and the accountants said that BCCI's deviousness outwitted them.

But is it possible that the financial authorities knew about BCCI's antics all along, but were, to put it bluntly, nobbled by the security services who used the bank as a window on the movement of terrorists funds, the arms trade, drugs traffickers and the like? Given that security services have already accepted that they paid operatives secretly through BCCI, this looks increasingly likely.

Investigators, spearheaded by the New York District Attorney's office, are now looking down every avenue for explanations for the regulators' relaxed attitude to BCCI. For example, they question whether there might be political corruption and have looked at a company where Brent Scowcroft, the President's foreign affairs adviser, was a director, and this may yet throw up other leads to the White House.

There are also indications that associates of the closed bank are now trying hard to cover their tracks. Kamal Adham, the former Saudi security adviser, is calling in some of the favours he gave to old friends in the top political echelons over the last nineteen years in a bid to restrain the investigation of his affairs. With his virtually bottomless pocket, he has hired a number of important policemen and lawyers to represent his case for keeping the lid on BCCI. He is also threatening to reveal uncomfortable facts about US covert operations, such as Irangate and the funding by Arab countries of the anti-Soviet Mujaheddin in Afghanistan. This may have had some success because US regional investigations into BCCI have been brought under the wing of the US Justice Department which has gained an understandable reputation for being soft on BCCI. But Adham's efforts have now been exposed because he tried to offer a young former aide of White House chief of staff John Sununu no less than $600,000 to join his lobbying team. The story leaked to the press and the aide resigned.

The reasons for the Bank of England's reluctance to act are equally hard to fathom. As early as 1978 the Bank appears to have suspected that something was wrong when it refused BCCI a full banking licence, but allowed BCCI to expand chaotically virtually unsupervised. Later, in 1984, the Bank cold-shouldered the Luxembourg authorities who were concerned about the bank's lack of regulation. The Bank waited another three years before starting to probe BCCI using BCCI's own auditors, Price Waterhouse, as investigators. Price Waterhouse then produced no less than ten increasingly critical reports before the country's prime regulator took BCCI to task. When the Bank of England finally moved to close BCCI on July 5 1991, it was seen as a rushed bid to pre-empt embarrassment rather than the considered response of a prime banking regulator. The consequences of New York district attorney Robert Morgenthau unveiling the damning results of his two-year investigation into the BCCI fraud before the Bank had taken any decisive action would have been damaging indeed.

The charge that the Bank of England failed to take 'appropriate and timely' action will be scrutinised by the Bingham inquiry. But its proceedings are being conducted in private, and its results may never be fully published. This confirms some suspicions that a cover-up is intended. But if negligence is established, heads must roll.

The role of Price Waterhouse, one of the world's top accountancy firms, also needs examining. As BCCI's second-string auditors, it pored over the books of

BCCI's Cayman company for a full thirteen years without so much as a murmur. In 1985, they looked at bogus treasury transactions and interpreted them as incompetence that could be corrected internally. It took them another six years to establish to the Bank of England's satisfaction that they had a massive fraud on their hands. Could self interest have got the better of their duty to the bank's shareholders and management or may it even have been pressure from some senior authority?

The grounds for believing there was a strong security interest in the bank are powerful. Bert Lance, in his evidence to a Senate committee, described BCCI as 'the bank of the CIA' and said he was visited by agents as early as 1981 and questioned about the bank's involvement in Irangate. The following year, a British accountant living in Geneva gave British diplomatic staff documentary evidence that he had been asked by the bank to participate in an arms deal. The embassy warned him even then that he was dealing with dangerous men. The most dangerous man of all, Abu Nidal, even maintained an account in one of the main London branches in the early eighties. The value of keeping open this window on the seedy secret world may have been irresistible. Was the Bank of England obliged to listen to this section of the community rather than its own regulatory voices, who were calling for action much earlier?

If there is good reason for this suspicion, BCCI's hundreds of thousands of depositors worldwide were left in the dark, while the spies and spooks had a field day. Tales abound of businesses that have gone bust, with lives shattered, and hard-earned savings wiped out. Despite the Sheikh's decision in October 1991 to abandon a rescue package in the UK, some still cling to the hope of compensation when the negligence is finally nailed.

This is the human dimension of financial fraud which can be overlooked when considering the larger and more nebulous forces that are bent on abusing banks. The lesson of BCCI is that the banking system and the men who police it need to be re-enforced. If BCCI is not to be repeated, the financial system and those who trust in it must be protected by its political masters from interference, and rules designed to catch men with Agha Hasan Abedi's talent to deceive must be rewritten. If that happens something will be salvaged from the BCCI débâcle.

# 1 The Making of Abedi

In 1946, the year before the last Viceroys of India, Lords Wavell and Mountbatten, put the finishing touches to the Partition of India a young trainee joined the Habib Bank in Bombay. The son of a Lucknow landlord who was estates manager to the Rajah of Mahmoodabad, Agha Hasan Abedi was well educated, with a degree in English literature, philosophy and law from his home town Islamic university. It was decided that he should start not as an ordinary bank trainee but as a 'selective service officer' – commission material rather than from the ranks.

When the bank moved to Karachi in 1947, following Partition and the establishment of Pakistan, Abedi went with it. He had already made his mark. Colleagues describe Abedi as a good marketing man and a persuasive talker, correct and polite. A keen developer of new business, he was willing to do all the early spade-work to bring in new clients and was quickly promoted to become head of the development department.

Apart from his work expanding the business, Abedi's passions were Indian classical music and his religion. He was a devout Shi'ite Muslim, abstaining from alcohol and leading a modest personal life. His first marriage was arranged. Later, as he became a powerful businessman, Abedi moved from traditional Islam to the Islamic offshoot philosophy of Sufism, and he used the Sufist charm and charisma outlawed by traditional Islam to mystify his followers both inside and outside the bank with suggestions of infallibility and self-sacrifice. To reinforce the Sufi effect, he would tell colleagues that his great-grandfather had come from the Persian religious town of Om, and his great-grandmother was born in Nishalbur, the home of the Omar Khayyam. One loyal friend was quoted as saying, 'He is the epitome of the high Muslim culture of India . . . there is no personal scandal about him, and he would never speak ill of anyone.'

The puritan religious ethic for hard work infected others, and the people Abedi worked with were driven to spend very long hours at the bank. He was not interested in a social life. In fact the closest he came to socialising was at conferences where he would spend long hours meeting clients.

'He kept a certain distance from the people who worked in the bank. On the other hand he was much more open than most presidents because he didn't lead a social life at all,' said Nadir Rahim, Abedi's head of human resources at BCCI. 'He was dedicated to the bank to the point that when you left at nine-thirty or ten at night he was still there, doing other things, making plans. He would say, "All right, I think I have given all of you enough time, now I must get on with what I am doing."'

Abedi's banking career progressed rapidly and promotions followed swiftly. First, he was made manager of the Rawalpindhi branch, then he won the prestigious posting to Lahore, the important provincial capital. He discovered that the secret of building banking business was making contacts, and after five or six years he had developed a formidable list of these.

One contact that he had cultivated as early as the mid-1950s was the Saigols – Pakistan's wealthiest textile family, and a major political force in the country. At this time, they wanted to boost their operations in Quetta, Baluchistan, and decided on flotation as a public company. They needed guidance and turned to their helpful bank manager, Abedi. The Saigols asked the Habib Bank if it would release him and, anxious to please a valued customer, in the manner of the region, the bank agreed. The secondment eventually became permanent. (A less flattering version of Abedi's parting from Habib suggests that he had extended loans to the Saigols much beyond what was proper, and he was told to leave.)

Abedi gained considerable respect for his successful handling of the Saigol flotation, and within eighteen months he had persuaded the Saigols that they should help him start a new bank. They committed 10 million rupees to the venture and the United Bank was launched in 1959 with the Saigols as virtually sole owners.

The launch of United was characterised by Abedi's special flair for big names and influence. Thus he appointed the former Prime Minister of Pakistan, I. I. Chundrigar, as chairman of the United board in the expectation that this would help him to get close to the new leader of Pakistan, General Mohammed Ayub Khan, who had come to power in a bloodless coup in 1958.

Given free rein to expand, Abedi turned his sights on the international scene. The Islamic Republic of Pakistan had a natural political as well as religious tie with the Arab world, and Abedi sought to exploit it to the full. In targeting the under-developed Gulf, he may also have detected the first signs of the oil rush that would occur over the next decade.

The Gulf was a region in a state of considerable flux. At the time when Abedi made his first visit to scout out the possibility of setting up a joint venture, in the mid-1960s, it was a group of tiny emirates ruled by local chieftains. Abedi approached the emir of the largest of the group, Abu Dhabi, but got the cold shoulder. Sheikh Shakbut rejected Abedi on the advice of the British Bank of the Middle East which said that the region did not need another bank. Shakbut had a reputation for miserliness in any event. One story has it that during the time that Abedi was still courting him, the Sheikh woke at four in the morning and demanded to see the money he had invested in Abedi's United Bank. Then he wanted breakfast.

Sheikh Shakbut's younger brother Zayed became increasingly aware of the damage his brother was inflicting on the nascent country, and on 6 August 1966, backed by a group of British officers, he overthrew Shakbut in a peaceful coup. The new sheikh was altogether more open to foreign influence. He later asserted command over the seven emirates of the region, and in 1971 formed the United Arab Emirates.

Both Pakistani banks now focused their attention on the new sheikh. Setting up a branch in his country was an invaluable way to tap into the oil money that was beginning to appear. It was also a launch-pad for moving out into other oil-rich Arab countries. But attracting the attention of Sheikh Zayed required some unusual tactics. The Sheikh's closest contact with Pakistan was not via conventional diplomatic channels, but through hunting with falcons and sand bustards, a sport in which his reputation was high. The travel writer Wilfred Thesiger met Sheikh Zayed as a young man when he spent most of his time in the al-Ain oasis, and wrote of him and his bedouin followers: 'He had a great reputation among the Bedu. . . . They said admiringly, "Zayed is a Bedu. He knows about camels, can ride like one of us, can shoot and knows how to fight."'

Soon after seizing power, Sheikh Zayed decided to go on an expedition to Pakistan and sent a cable to the Habib Bank which had already been in touch with its own plans for a joint venture, saying he was interested in coming over to Baluchistan to hunt with his birds of prey. The Habib Bank responded by saying it could promise nothing better than shooting and deer hunting. But when Abedi heard about Zayed's plans, he immediately fired off a cable: 'Excellent falconry here. Don't worry, I can fix everything up.'

The visit to Pakistan led to some absurd rivalry for the Sheikh's attention and business. When Zayed and his party were about to arrive at Karachi airport for the start of the trip, both Abedi and the managing director of the Habib Bank lined up on the apron to greet him. The Pakistan government's chief of protocol was horrified. Whose guest was the Sheikh supposed to be? Both bankers claimed the honour. When Zayed landed, the chief of protocol said he would let him decide. But the Sheikh was tired after his journey and accepted the invitation to rest at the government guest-house, courtesy of the Pakistan government, until he had made up his mind.

The party set off in convoy to the guest-house where the bankers simply had to wait until the Sheikh surfaced. The wait was a long one and eventually the managing director of the Habib Bank departed, leaving a disgruntled message that the Sheikh could contact him when he was ready. When Sheikh Zayed awoke and summoned the bankers, only Abedi was still waiting to welcome him to Pakistan. United won the day.

Nothing was too much trouble for Abedi who personally supervised every last detail of the visit, impressing the Sheikh and winning kudos. The story goes that on another visit by the Sheikh, each of the two banks had lined up a bouquet of flowers which Zayed would receive when he arrived at the airport. The United Bank's representative, upset that his bouquet was smaller than Habib's switched the name tags when the opposition wasn't looking.

In 1967 the Pakistani leader Ayub Khan decided to invite Sheikh Zayed for a state visit. Abedi was in charge of the Pakistani end of the arrangements and he suggested to Khan that it might be a fine gesture to give the Sheikh a horse. Zayed was covered with embarrassment since he had nothing with which to reciprocate. In the twinkling of a falcon's eye, Abedi extended his wrist, slipped off his diamond-encrusted Rolex watch which the Sheikh had presented him some time earlier and indicated he should present it to Ayub Khan. Honour was restored and Abedi had crept up another rung in the Sheikh's estimation. These gestures eventually paid off for Abedi, as Sheikh Zayed allowed United to open its first branches in Abu Dhabi, several years ahead of the Habib Bank. BCCI's protocol department was to become celebrated along the same lines – providing all the creature comforts that important clients could desire.

Abedi had now achieved a foothold in a country that was to undergo a most extraordinary transformation. By the late 1960s the oil-pumping had begun, and Zayed had become one of the world's richest men. The cultural and emotional shock to any individual suddenly transformed in a few brief years from a man happy to enjoy the simplicity of a picnic of dried fish wrapped in newspaper to an Arab Croesus must have been enormous. Sheikh Zayed had little experience of exposure to the outside world – indeed, his literacy and numeracy are believed to be limited – but now he was being pursued for his wealth by some very sophisticated operators whom he had no means to repel.

The newly enriched Sheikh began to travel, and Abedi established a protocol department at United Bank to look after his every whim. Abedi also helped him to acquire residences all over the world. For his occasional visits to London, he established a base in the fashionable Boltons in South Kensington. Zayed, who is thought to have fourteen wives and more than forty children, housed his harem across the square from his home in a luxurious white mansion with gilded gates. He cut a strange figure emerging into that genteel corner of London.

Sheikh Zayed needed a team to assist him to manage his vast wealth. In 1981 he appointed Ghanim Faris al-Mazrui to the position of 'chairman/director general of the department of personal affairs of HRH ruler of Abu Dhabi and chairman of the Abu Dhabi Investment Authority'. Mazrui, who was also the Sheikh's representative on the board of BCCI, continues today to head up Sheikh Zayed's personal office.

With Abu Dhabi under his thumb, Abedi now looked to Saudi Arabia for a connection. Both he and the Habib Bank had applied to the governor of the Saudi Monetary Agency, Mr Anwar Ali, for permission to open up in Jeddah. They were both turned down. Once again, however, Abedi's brilliant opportunism and ring of informers came into play. He heard that the Saudi royal family had written to General Yahya Khan (who had just overthrown Ayub), thanking him for his support of the Arab cause and asking him if there was anything they could do in return. In normal circumstances Khan would have declined politely. But Abedi knew that Khan had a weakness, and he played on this. There is an apocryphal story that Abedi ensured that a letter asking the royal family of Saudi Arabia to grant United permission to set up a branch was put in front of Khan when he was the worse for drink. The request was granted immediately and the first United branch was opened in Dharan. The Habib Bank complained bitterly, but Anwar Ali neatly explained that he had only refused permission for a branch in Jeddah, not in Dharan.

Abedi had taken considerable advantage of his political connections in Pakistan, and this told against him later. In 1972 there was a change of regime and Zulfiqar Ali Bhutto took over from Ayub Khan. Bhutto, a socialist, was no friend of the Pakistani banking system in general, nor of Abedi's United Bank in particular. His programme included nationalisation of the banks, and Abedi had to make plans.

Abedi was also falling out with the Saigols at this time. Some claim that they were over-borrowing from their own bank and that Abedi was resisting. The family wanted him replaced but faced an almost complete mutiny from Abedi's devoted staff. To forestall the Saigols, Abedi went to Ghulam Ishaq Khan, the president of the Pakistan State Bank, who used his good offices to keep Abedi in place. Ishaq Khan subsequently became head of the BCCI Foundation, Abedi's 'charitable fund'. Today, Ishaq Khan is the president of Pakistan.

With the writing on the wall at United, Abedi began planning for the setting-up of a bank where he would have the controlling stake. He went to his old and trusted contact Sheikh Zayed with a request that he repay with hard cash the help Abedi had given to him on the many occasions he had come to Pakistan on hunting expeditions. The Sheikh seems to have obliged him with the $2.5 million he needed, but other sources indicate that the Saudi businessman Kamal Adham, another subsequent supporter, and Bank of America may have lent Abedi the money. Bhutto said later that he believed Abedi stole the $2.5 million from United Bank, perhaps by creating some phoney loans using the system which he subsequently applied on a grand scale.

The preparations for the new bank also included finding a major American backer. Abedi went first to American Express who were impressed by his credentials with the Gulf Arabs and prepared to back him. However, they wanted some management control which Abedi was not prepared to grant.

The Pakistani then went to Bank of America (BoA), whom he knew and whom he had already done a good turn. This occurred when BoA was seeking to establish itself in Pakistan and needed a network of branches where its customers could have drawing facilities. BoA had approached Habib, who refused, and they then turned to United, who agreed. A little later Abedi had also helped the American bank in a small but significant way. The first branch of the new BoA bank was opened on the first floor of a building in Karachi directly above United Bank, but the architects said the joists would not bear the weight of the BoA safe. Abedi solved their problem by providing a corner where BoA could put its safe.

When BoA agreed to take a 40 per cent stake in the fledgling bank, the final piece of the jigsaw fell into place for the international bank that Abedi had dreamed of for so long. On 21 September 1972 the Bank of Credit and Commerce International was registered in Luxembourg, founded by Agha Hasan Abedi – with more than a little help from his friends. When Bhutto heard about the creation of the new bank, he had Abedi's passport confiscated. Winning it back took all Abedi's powers of persuasion. For example he persuaded Sheikh Zayed to set up a charitable foundation in Pakistan, to build a hospital in Lahore and start two newspapers in Bhutto's Sindh province. Abedi had also begun making friends in Iran, and the Shah of Iran's brother, Prince Mahmood Reza Pahlavi, is thought to have interceded on his behalf.

Abedi was now talking about creating the biggest bank in the world. His achievement in building United Bank into the second largest in Pakistan was considered as little short of a miracle, and when he regaled his colleagues with his expansionary plans for BCCI they believed him and wanted to be part of them. He would tell them he was a visionary and urged them all to project themselves into the future. Nadir Rahim, who had known Abedi since he was a child, recalls 'how he started collecting a team that he thought would take it forward because he already had a very specific plan for it to become an international bank, a Third World bank, a Third World voice'.

To attain this objective, the bank was supposed to provide a link between the oil surplus countries, the industrially and technologically developed countries and the developing countries of the Third World, through a network of commercial and international banking branches and units. Abedi also proclaimed a set of ethical principles governing the use of the bank's profits. He said they should be split three ways: one-third for charity, one-third for staff benefits and one-third for promotional activities. Rahim says that 'The management group and the shareholders of the new bank eventually agreed to provide for a minority shareholding by means of a trust which was established for the benefit of staff, and a foundation which would provide aid and services for global deserving causes.' It was left unclear what the deserving causes should be. But by no definition could they include the people who eventually got their hands on that money.

# 2 Going for Growth: a Tale of Two Brothers

United Bank of Pakistan presented Agha Hasan Abedi with the opportunity to build a bank in his own image, but owned by somebody else. Setting up the Bank of Credit and Commerce International enabled Abedi to own his own bank, though exactly how much would always be shrouded in mystery.

His team at the new bank would be very similar to that at the old one. Mesmerised by his success and personality, they had eagerly climbed aboard the new Abedi business. They were not only happy working with each other professionally, there was also a social coherence stemming from their similar backgrounds.

Abedi's team were for the most part Mahojars – the Urdu word for immigrants – and they had come from India to Pakistan at the time of Partition. The very fact that the native Pakistanis dubbed them immigrants in this way, suggests the instability of their position. Insecure in their new home and rather clannish, the Mahojars took the route of so many new immigrant groups and worked extremely hard to build prosperity. It is little wonder that they set up their own political party in Pakistan, which in recent years has become quite powerful – it contributed to the overthrow of Benazir Bhutto.

Although the bank was registered in Luxembourg, Abedi decided to put down its roots in London. He was not welcome in Pakistan at the time, and given that English was the second language of all of the bank's leading officers, the British financial centre was most comfortable for him. It was also already regarded as leniently regulated. From then on, there was a steady flow of Pakistanis to London to join the portentously named Central Support Organisation.

The bank made a point of not giving its staff titles, but this does not mean that BCCI was a flat organisation. In fact it appears to have been extremely hierarchical. There was no question about who gave the orders and when they must be obeyed. Agha Hasan Abedi had the honorific of president, and even if he liked to mix with the great and the good, and to operate in a spiritual plane outside the routine operations of the bank, his finger was on every pulse and his hand in every deal.

But Abedi would not move unless his faithful and brilliant lieutenant said so. Swaleh Naqvi devised the banking systems and kept the internal books. He seems to have been relatively unimpressed by the Abedi rhetoric – his interest was to get the mechanics of the bank functioning. He was a quite brilliant banker, 'very creative and inventive in devising projects', said one former client who later had cause to regret it. Abedi was totally in awe of Naqvi's brainpower, and there is no evidence that Naqvi ever failed to get his way, because he knew exactly how to present information to ensure that Abedi gave his signature to a deal.

Later, when Abedi was ill, Naqvi took over as president, and once his collection of 6,500 neatly handwritten files was found in Abu Dhabi, it was clear that some of the bank's more extraordinary accounting and banking procedures were of his devising.

However, Naqvi stepped into the number two position only after Abedi's former favourite left at the end of the 1970s. Abdul Sami came with Abedi from

United, where he was Abedi's deputy, and went to lead the assault on America. Having set up the acquisitions of the National Bank of Georgia and Financial General, he expected to be put in charge of the entire US operation. But Abedi appears to have preferred Roy Carlson, who had formerly been with Bank of America, for the job, and Sami left with a $400,000 pay-off.

From that point on, Abedi and Naqvi completely masterminded the progress of the bank. The rest of the staff were functionaries, operating at the beck and call of Abedi and Naqvi. The example set by the departure of Sami was to resound through the bank, and anyone who displayed individuality or held a different point of view from the president knew that his days were numbered. This highly autocratic, personality-based structure opened the way for abuse and secrecy.

The ranks of loyal supporters grew quickly. To some degree they split between Abedi's men and Naqvi's. The president, for example, used Dildar Rezvi to organise hospitality, which meant escorting Abedi's many guests around the world, with money no object. Mohammed Hafiz, the company secretary and monitor of the BCCI share register, also waited loyally on Abedi.

A number of financial men answered first to Naqvi. His list of retainers was headed by Mohammed Azmatullah, who helped him manage his secret files. Azmatullah controlled all contact between Naqvi and the outside world. Saleem Sidiqi, who had headed the international section at United Bank of Pakistan, led the inspection department, and is said to have kept files on everyone at the bank. Ameer Siddiki was head of the credit committee, Imtiaz Ahmed was head of the credit division, and the finance director was Masihur Rahman.

The international managers were swapped around as the bank developed its operations overseas. Probably the most important job was that of head of the UK operation. In the early days this post was held by Velayat Husain Abedi, and latterly by Basheer Chowdry, who ran the UK operation until it was closed down. Nazir Chinoy was in charge of the French operation until his arrest for participating in drugs money laundering in 1988. As the bank grew it developed regional heads like Nadir Rahim who took charge of the small Indian operation. Iqbal Rizvi seemed the highest-flyer on the international circuit. He started as a minor functionary in Iran, moved to France and steadily acquired more responsibility until he was in charge of Europe, Africa and South America.

In 1972 Abedi had a team, a piece of paper from Luxembourg proving the bank was registered, and $2.5 million of issued capital. Now he needed to find premises, attract accounts and above all expand the business.

Given the close ties of President Abedi with the Sheikh of Abu Dhabi and the bank's Muslim culture, it was natural for him to focus his attention on attracting business from other Arab countries. The importance of the Arab connection was made clear in 1978, when Abedi gave *Euromoney* magazine a list of shareholders in the bank. These included the ruling families of Bahrain, Sharjah, Abu Dhabi, Dubai, Saudi Arabia and Iran. But there is no evidence that major members of the royal families had more than token stakes.

Indeed, some of the thirty-nine Arab dignitaries who appear as shareholders in 1979 doubtless acquired their stakes in the same way as the Shah of Iran's brother,

Prince Mahmood Reza, obtained his – as a gift from Abedi and Naqvi, who were keen to build up a distinguished letterhead to impress and bamboozle. That early shareholder list contains five members of the Al-Nahyan family of Abu Dhabi; Sheikh Zayed has a mere 0.47 per cent and his son Sheikh Khalifa has 1.24 per cent. Ali Shorafa, who was Sheikh Zayed's director for presidential affairs, and an original investor in the shadowy Credit and Commerce American Holdings (CCAH) company, has just 0.44 per cent. Small stakes are also held by Saudis Prince Salman and Prince Naif. The stakes of Saudi businessman Ghaith Pharaon and his son Wabel, on the other hand, come to over 15 per cent, and these are the largest shareholdings outside the BCCI-owned International Credit and Investment Company (ICIC). Swaleh Naqvi appears with a token 0.03 per cent.

One early investor was Union Bank of Switzerland through a holding company, Thesaurus Continental Securities Corporation. In 1976, UBS sold the Geneva-based Banque de Commerce et Placements to BCCI but kept a 15 per cent stake which was held by Thesaurus. BCP was later an important BCCI laundry for Noriega's drugs money. Thesaurus was the conduit for secret South African government funds used to buy the *Citizen* newspaper in Johannesburg, a scandal which became known as Muldergate, after the South African information minister, Connie Mulder.

The Abu Dhabi connection, built up since the 1960s through the personal connection of Abedi and the Sheikh, carried little weight with the rest of the wealthy Arab world. It seemed that the Arab countries either would not grasp Abedi's concept of the Muslim bank or were worried about the men who were propagating it. In any event, the countries in the Gulf Cooperation Council were less helpful than Abedi had hoped they would be. In Saudi Arabia, for example, he had powerful friends, like Kamal Adham and Ghaith Pharaon, but the King resolutely refused BCCI permission even to set up a finance company. Bahrain and Qatar were equally inhospitable. Kuwait allowed Abedi a 49 per cent shareholding in a finance company, Kuwait International Finance Company (KIFCO), but no bank, and Oman permitted a 29 per cent shareholding in National Bank of Oman.

The failure to push deeply into the Arab world made success in London all the more vital. The bank was starting from absolute rock bottom. One salesman said there were 'no accounts, no activity, no furniture in the bank. It was desperate, we were visiting hotels and jumping on Arabs to get them to open accounts, no matter what they wanted to put in.'

Everyone brought into the bank at this stage was harnessed to the relentless drive for accounts. The growth when it came would be stunning, expanding from the modest $2.5 million capital in 1972 to a worldwide operation stretching through more than seventy countries, with 400 branches and a capital base of $23 billion at the end. But in the early days, to say that the atmosphere was frenetic would be an understatement. As one executive working at BCCI shortly after the launch put it, 'They expected you to be running in the street seven days a week until midnight. Every account was being constantly reviewed and your performance against target constantly monitored.' Meeting and beating targets were rewarded by a mention in the bank magazine; top achievers would receive a letter from President Abedi. The speed of BCCI's growth would eventually attract the attention of the Bank of England in 1978 who ordered a halt when the number of branches in the United Kingdom reached forty-five.

Eventually this fever of activity began to produce rewards as the bank's Muslim message found its way to a number of communities who had money, and for the five years between 1975 and 1980, BCCI grew into a bank of substance both in the United Kingdom and globally. Now the City of London had to sit up. For years they assumed that Abedi was a man of no importance and that his parvenu immigrant bank would go nowhere. So they ignored him and refused his requests for meetings. He felt excluded from the 'Club', as he was later to call the City of London.

The turning-point came when BCCI took over the 101 Leadenhall Street premises in the heart of the City. Abedi could no longer be completely ignored, and his requests for meetings were answered. Those City doubters who remained could not overlook another consideration: the world was awash with Arab petrodollars and the City was in hot competition for Arab business with Paris, New York and even Tokyo. BCCI's shareholders and links with the Arab world put them in a pole position to win that business. It was accepted that as long as BCCI kept to that sort of business, they should not be investigated too closely.

BCCI made hay out of the London connection. Arabs from the newly enriched Gulf states came to the UK to enjoy the casinos, buy property, educate their children, shop and race their horses, and they banked in droves at BCCI branches in their favoured prosperous locations in London – Marble Arch, Kensington, Mayfair and so on. Between 1973 and 1977 the number of BCCI branches in the United Kingdom grew from four to forty-five, and in the United Arab Emirates from eight to twenty-nine. The worldwide branch network expanded from nineteen to 146. In 1973 BCCI was operating in five countries and by 1977 it was represented in thirty-two.

Every financial ratio used reflects this growth. BCCI's assets grew ten-fold, from $200 million to $2.2 billion, its capital from $5 million to $113 million, its deposits from $19 million to $2 billion and its profits from $335,000 to $25 million. These were figures that left some bankers gasping and others highly suspicious.

Ghassan Qassem, one of BCCI's top branch managers in London, says that 'Top people, such as members of royal families, came and opened accounts in those days. So did leaders from Nigeria, Syria, Iraq.' Qassem's *entrée* to the fabulous funds of the Saudi Arabian royal family came via the manager of the funds of Prince Faisal, a cousin of King Fayed. Qassem was told that the Prince was staying in his residence near Hampstead Heath and that he should visit him the same day. Apparently Prince Faisal had horses and property in the United Kingdom and needed the funds for their upkeep managed. Qassem, a Jordanian, established instant rapport with the Prince, and eventually brought in the accounts of four of his brothers.

The helter-skelter quest for accounts led the bank to abuse procedures, says Qassem. 'They made the staff open an account for anyone, just for the sake of reaching targets. They never went through proper opening procedures, and that was an invitation for crooks to join the bank.'

The bank flourished by handling large numbers of overseas accounts for private individuals, many of whom had rather more doubtful reasons to be storing their money in the United Kingdom than the Saudis' need to fund the upkeep of their estates and horses. BCCI attracted powerful individuals who needed somewhere to secrete their wealth away from the prying eyes of their countries' tax or law enforcement authorities. 'Flight capital' of this kind came from places like Nigeria, Panama and Peru, and was welcomed by the bank that could afford to ask no questions.

BCCI also set up a special operation for the large quantities of illegal cash which moved between the Indian sub-continent and the UK. This system is widely known as Hundi or Hawalla and its primary aim is to break rules on the export of foreign exchange. The global Chinese community has a similar system called Chitty banking. These are age-old practices which traditionally use corner-shops and family networks, but BCCI developed it to a fine art. At its simplest, the bank arranged for a deposit in the local currency at one end and a withdrawal in a different currency at the other, without audit trail or paperwork. More sophisticated versions of this system would be applied to the needs of the money launderer and the international arms trader.

The bank also sold itself to traders who needed letters of credit to speed up the transfer of funds across the world. This was to become a very substantial business for a number of Asian traders who found in the bank kindred spirits prepared to take trade finance a lot further than is conventionally possible. Foremost among these traders were the three Gokal brothers, whose Gulf Shipping Group took BCCI for such a ride that its outstanding borrowings of $1 billion-plus may ultimately have been the primary cause of the bank's downfall.

Yet another form of business would soon get the bank into deep waters. This was the massive lines of credit it opened up to governments round the world who were having difficulty with the traditional sovereign lenders. Abedi had set up the bank with a Third World image which gave him a ready-made *entrée* into the treasuries and political powerhouses of many Third World countries. Abedi curried favour with politicians by offering lavish hospitality and eventually succeeded in persuading a number of governments in Africa and South America to fill a hole in their balance of payments by taking a loan from BCCI rather than from the International Monetary Fund or the World Bank. Investigations have already begun in Peru and Nigeria into alleged bribery of officials by BCCI.

The development of customer business was one building-brick for the bank's survival. But Abedi and Naqvi had to ensure that they could control the shareholdings in the bank itself, so that they could keep money coming in from the Gulf to build up the capital while they retained controlling stakes. This meant seeking other locations where BCCI's finances and shareholdings could be recorded away from the prying eyes of UK or even Luxembourg regulators. One route towards creating a market in BCCI shares would have been to take the company on to a stock exchange, but that would have required opening up the ownership of BCCI shares to public scrutiny, which would certainly have been resisted by some of the bank's more shadowy backers. The individual likely to resist most would have been Abedi himself, who claimed for many years to control the ownership of BCCI.

The bank therefore embarked on a course of developing a network of offshore companies. These could have had the effect of obscuring ownership and control. Later it was arranged for a second company to operate in parallel to the Luxembourg-registered BCCI Holdings company.

In 1976 BCCI formed a parallel company, sometimes called the bank within the bank, based in the Cayman Islands. Abedi would later claim that there was no connection between this parallel company, ICIC, and BCCI. Even now sources close to Abedi maintain that 'There was no link between BCCI and ICIC except that ICIC (Overseas) lent against shares of BCCI. In some cases where the shareholders were not able to repay the advance for a long time, it was even selling the shares.' In fact the BCCI bank company would use its shadow company ICIC to make loans to shareholders to enable them to hold on to their shares, or to indemnify them against any losses. BCCI also borrowed against its own shares. This happened when Bank of America wanted to dispose of its 24 per cent holding in 1980. Using its ICIC network, BCCI took out a loan with Bank of America to the value of the shares which it was selling.

The Federal Reserve indictment makes the connection between BCCI and ICIC very clear when it states, 'ICIC Overseas operated under the control of and at the direction of senior BCCI management, including Abedi and Naqvi, to further the business interests of BCCI, and acted as the *alter ego* or agent for BCCI in connection with the acquisition of CCAH [the vehicle used to buy First American] and a number of other transactions. . . . The two groups generally operated as a single entity.'

The sheer similarity of the names and the complexity of the arrangements create suspicion, even without the luxury of a detailed examination of balance sheets and company records which Cayman law precludes. For example, BCCI (Overseas), based in the Cayman Islands, is 100 per cent owned by BCCI Holdings in Luxembourg. The senior Cayman company is a UK charity, called ICIC Foundation, which owns an investment company, ICIC Foundation (Cayman), which owns 35 per cent of BCCI's Geneva-based bank, Banque de Commerce et Placements (the rest was owned by BCCI Holdings SA and Union Bank of Switzerland). ICIC Foundation was also an investor in BCCI; it borrowed $74 million from its sister company, ICIC (Overseas), to acquire 9 per cent of BCCI shares.

Other Cayman investors in BCCI Holdings are the mysteriously named ICIC Staff Benefit Trust and the ICIC Staff Benefit Fund. These may have had a rationale for Abedi and Naqvi, but the rest of the staff found that they had been milked dry when it came to redundancy benefits.

By the late 1970s the curious personality-based management structure, the questionable basis for the bank's growth and the unfathomable nature of the offshore web of companies had not escaped the notice of regulators and backers alike. The Bank of England appeared ready to admit that there was a question-mark over the bank when it refused to grant it a licence in 1978, and yet in May that year, *Forbes* magazine described BCCI as 'unquestionably the most successful newcomer to Arab banking in London'. At the time Abedi said in an interview given to *Euromoney*, 'The Bank of England probably hasn't given permission because of the atmosphere surrounding BCCI and the propaganda that has been spread about us. . . . It's not only the Bank of England that is against us, but the Club.'

Previous fans at Bank of America, who in the early days had been willing to back Abedi's freewheeling management style, were also getting cold feet about the bank's rapid rate of growth in the late 1970s. This leading institution had begun as an enthusiastic backer, with a 40 per cent stake, but it had allowed its holding to decline over the years by not taking up rights issues. It produced a critical report on BCCI's management of its loans in August 1978, and in June 1980 sold the 24 per cent remaining, saying it had established its own presence in the Middle East. In fact it had become concerned about the BCCI style and wanted nothing more to do with it.

The shareholding of Bank of America had given BCCI an early respectability on which to build growth. The other building-brick in the early construction of BCCI came from the Gokal brothers, who were among its first major customers and growing like topsy, primarily from business in the Gulf.

The Gokals were more than just BCCI's biggest customers, they were also brother Shi'ites and fellow Pakistanis. Both the Gokals' Gulf Shipping and Abedi's BCCI were led by charismatic, all-powerful individuals and both shared a culture of opulence and optimism. They would travel very similar courses over nineteen years, booming in tandem and declining together. Indeed, the Gokals' main holding company, Gulf International Holdings SA, went into 'controlled management' or administration on 3 July 1991, just two days before BCCI was closed.

The Gokals' is another story of growth from unlikely beginnings. The Gokal family have their origins in Gujarat and, like another great Pakistani business family, the

Saigols, are Khojas, or converts to Islam. In the wake of Partition, the Gokals moved to Iraq and initially the family prospered. They had a trading business in Basra which became the largest world exporter of dates, and a religious member of the family arranged transport for pilgrims on the Hajj, the pilgrimage to Mecca.

Tragedy hit the Gokals in 1969 when the uncle of the three brothers who now run the business was hanged in Iraq following an accusation from a business competitor – later proved unfounded – that he was an Israeli agent. The younger generation fled the country for their lives. The eldest brother, Mustafa, went to Pakistan where he set up Gulf Shipping and Trading, while the middle brother, Abbas, established a shipping company in London. Within three years Abbas was exporting great quantities of cement to the Gulf, where a building boom had started in earnest, as well as to Nigeria and India. For five years Abbas's companies built up the world's largest fleet of some 300 ships. In 1976 Abbas moved his business over to Geneva to avoid having to pay UK taxation.

Abbas was undoubtedly the family entrepreneur. A workaholic who put twenty hours a day into the company, he had a charismatic presence as well as a quick brain. Abbas Gokal also had a very strong nerve, and anybody who came to him with a problem went away believing that they themselves had caused it, and so would have to solve it. Abbas's elder brother Mustafa was a quite different personality. Deeply religious, he was none the less thrust into Pakistani politics by Agha Hasan Abedi who advised the president of Pakistan General al-Haq to appoint him as his shipping adviser.

The boom in the Gulf provided a growing market for the Gokal company, but the business also carved out a less savoury niche for itself in the shipping world, being prepared to take anything anywhere. For example, it set up a company, called Tradinaft, which is said to have broken sanctions and traded with South Africa. One of the best deals Gulf did in the mid-1970s was the shipment of tanks from the Eastern seaboard of the United States to Egypt. The arms were listed as 'industrial machinery' but they were loaded by the US army and discharged by the Egyptian army under a massive cloak of secrecy. In another escapade in international politics, it is understood that the Gokals employed Eddie Kamil, a former Seychelles minister of internal affairs, as its personnel manager for four years. In fact, his actual task was to organise the financing of a coup in the Seychelles. (This was subsequently attempted but failed.) The Gokals continue to own a number of hotels in the islands, as well as real estate.

During this period, Gulf worked closely and profitably with BCCI which was of course desperate for big customers and prepared to go to great lengths to accommodate their needs. Most Gulf ships were mortgaged by BCCI at extremely high and unrealistic valuations. BCCI also remortgaged many Gokal ships using inflated estimates. Staff were aware that BCCI was a friendly bank because of the informal way in which they were treated. One former Gulf employee relates, 'We used to go round to BCCI and pick up a bag of money to pay somebody off. I would go to 101 Leadenhall Street [the BCCI headquarters] and see a man called Shafiqur Rahman Khan. He would smile at me, and say, "Sign this piece of paper." I would write Mickey Mouse on a piece of tissue paper which was then thrown away. He handed me a bag of money which I would then take back and distribute.'

It appears that the early boom of the business went to Abbas Gokal's head; riding high on a business that seemed to promise infinite expansion, he entered areas quite outside his competence. For example, he entered the highly risky arena of futures and commodities trading and lost heavily. He became exposed to a rapidly rising yen and was losing heavily by the early 1980s.

The man Abbas Gokal put in charge of futures was a twenty-six-year-old brought in from Chicago on a salary of $480,000. He was given a completely free hand to wheel and deal. According to a colleague, 'When he lost money, he went on holiday, and when he made it, he traded it again until he lost it, and then he went on holiday.' At this time there was already talk of money disappearing from the company into employees' pockets.

Gokal also liked to encourage enterprise within his own family. It is said that he gave his son a Reuters machine and an active credit line of $100 million to learn the futures trading business.

There were other signs of uncoordinated diversification as well. For example, Gokal bought into Christian Dior and sold out at a loss. He also acquired a chain of butcher's shops which subsequently failed, and he took an interest in companies associated with UK designers Alistair Blair and Uzbeck.

By 1978, according to BCCI's auditors, Price Waterhouse, the Gulf companies were running into difficulties and their BCCI accounts needed some massaging. The 1991 Price Waterhouse report states: 'It appears that account manipulation began at this stage, and to this end a "special duties" department was set up to oversee these accounts. This was a full-time occupation which involved the manufacture of documentation, inflation of account turnover, concealment of fund flows, etc.'

This aspect of the Price Waterhouse report accords with perceptions on the ground. The management consensus in 1979 was that the business was in difficulty and needed to trim its sails. Late that year, a meeting of all the managers of the ship-broking offices was convened at Monte Carlo to discuss problems in the business. It lasted for two days, and it seemed to all present that there would be widespread redundancies and office closures. At the end of the second day, Abbas Gokal took the podium to deliver his closing speech. Its tone took all the managers by surprise. Instead of reflecting the downbeat mood of the meeting, he announced a major expansion of the business and the setting-up of a large number of offices in the Gulf and the Red Sea area.

According to one manager, Gokal left the meeting on the Sunday and went straight to Kuwait. He returned to Geneva on the following Tuesday with a cheque in his pocket for a reputed $1.4 billion. 'This was his first major influx of pure money, not money against mortgages or money against a particular deal. This time he went out and got pure money.' It was assumed at the time that the money came from BCCI.

Even by BCCI standards, the $1.4 billion figure seems excessive for this period, but sources close to BCCI admit that the relationship between Gulf and the bank changed dramatically at this time. They argue that the bank was concerned about its exposure to the Gokals, which currently stood at $80 million, and decided not to increase this beyond $100 million. However, they also claim that an officer of the bank was bribed and, acting without authority, issued a guarantee to the Gokals for an extension of the loan to $400 million. 'He did not pass the contingency and liability entries required when you issue a guarantee or letter of credit,' states the BCCI man. When the matter was uncovered, the officer joined the Gokals' company.

The increased line of credit had a dramatic effect on Abbas Gokal's personal style. 'Prior to that he had been a quiet man. Even though he mixed with princes he lived in a maisonette in Ealing [a middle-class London suburb], and he had a nice car, but it was obviously only for business. Then it all changed and he became flash. Instead of just one car, it was matching Rolls-Royces in Geneva and London. The office in Geneva was suddenly decorated by an expensive interior designer. His whole personality changed: from being quiet and introspective he became a Jack the Lad.' He also grew increasingly aloof from managers who had once found him approachable and open to new ideas.

The degree to which the shippers sank the bank remains a matter for conjecture. What is certain is that from an early stage the Gokals were not repaying their loans. The bank appeared not to insist on their repayment, and was prepared to doctor its books to show that they were still performing. Ultimately, those loans had assumed an untenable proportion of its balance-sheet and the cover-up was out of hand. According to the Price Waterhouse report circulated on 22 June 1991, over the fifteen years the Gokals banked with BCCI, they had 750 accounts, whose total turnover was $15 billion.

Gokal seems to have undergone the Abedi experience: uncontrolled growth fuelling disproportionate expectations, which could only be met by the creation of funny money. That, in time, would sink both their ships.

# 3 Mammon and Mohammed

BCCI was a quirky bank from day one and before. Its founders wanted to create an alternative culture to the traditional Western bank. They were not embarrassed about encouraging the practice of Islam during working hours; they consciously adopted a policy of recruiting practising Muslims; of course they favoured Arab and Muslim clients; and they used the rhetoric of Sufism and the charitable Giving which it advocated. The bank's Muslim culture had a powerful appeal for a religion which was feeling a surge of confidence, and for a people which had long felt oppressed and excluded from the commanding heights of the Western world.

The Islamic bond was a powerful motivator for employees who felt an unusual degree of loyalty to each other and to their inspirational masters. But the enthusiasm for all things Muslim also brought them into the company of some extremely unsavoury elements, such as international terrorist Abu Nidal, and the men organising the building of an Islamic bomb.

Islam may have been the predominant culture of the bank, but the last thing its founders were was naive or unmaterialistic. Although Agha Hasan Abedi is thought to have been a practising Muslim, there is plenty of evidence to show that he used the religion's rhetoric to his own ends. This confused faithful members of the staff as much as world leaders who thought they had at last found an ethical banker.

Professor Akbar Ahmed, the Muslim philosopher and Cambridge academic who wrote *Discovering Islam*, now part of Abedi's bedside reading, says the Eastern culture has a three-part social structure: loyalty, nepotism and hospitality. The bank took all these to extremes, which may be why it apparently failed to notice when its faith was being unmercifully exploited.

Abedi's loyalty to his staff and former friends was legendary, and he went out of his way to protect them. When a member of staff demanded unreasonable compensation, he would insist the lawyers paid him off. If a personnel mistake was made, instead of firing the individual concerned, he would demand that he be moved within the bank for the sake of his family, and not dismissed. As one friend put it, 'He believed in accountability, not punishability.'

Abedi was of course loyal to his financial backer, the Sheikh of Abu Dhabi, but Professor Ahmed says that the bond between them was that of brothers, and not just based on Abedi's self-interest. Zayed's respect for Abedi was to be demonstrated later when he was the first at his bedside after Abedi suffered a heart attack, and it followed that when Abedi needed help for his bank, Sheikh Zayed would agree without demur.

'Are we to see this, as some Western people might, as two shady characters who have got together and made a deal? No. What deal can a sheikh who is one of the richest men in the world do with a sick bank? What can he offer, except an obligation, code of behaviour?' Professor Ahmed asks.

Nepotism and the family are an extension of the loyalty principle, which is fine in personal life but can be fatal in a business context. The bank was an extended family and members were always found a job. Abedi employed General Zia's son when he knew full well it would pay handsome dividends in business terms, and Qassem took on chief financial officer Masihur Rahman's daughter even though he says she was a 'silly girl'. This all led to a philosophy of scratching backs as a matter of course. In Pakistan there is even a word for it, *sifarish*.

There was also the importance of hospitality. In the Arab world this is part and parcel of doing business. Abedi personally greeted the Sheikh of Abu Dhabi whenever the latter visited Pakistan, and he was prepared to sit for hours discussing hunting matters with a sheikh if in the end it meant assuming responsibility for his portfolio of shares. Business would not even be mentioned, but the unspoken agenda was always clear.

Doing business in this way meant that branches of the bank had to look more like a hotel or a home than an office. Abedi insisted that they were comfortable and positioned close to where his customers were. The BCCI look was distinctive – open-plan, of course, in the modern style. The president sat where all could see him and where he could be approached. The boardroom tables were round and Abedi deliberately sat at a different seat every time to avoid giving the impression of 'I am the boss and you are my workers'.

The buildings themselves were located at all the main city centres or in places where they would have maximum impact. One of the first buildings visitors arriving from London's Heathrow airport saw was BCCI's tall and imposing branch. BCCI's buildings were deliberately luxurious. This was a marketing ploy by Abedi who knew that wealthy customers were impressed by opulence and lavishness. There may also have been a sense that this *nouveau riche* institution had to be one up on the Joneses, or the Barclays.

A colleague of Abedi said that the consistency of the branches' appearance was another marketing ploy. 'Whether it was in the City of London or a place like

Yemen, you knew what to expect the BCCI branch to look like. A certain colour of plate glass. You knew there would be a certain desk. It was completely standard right through the world. That was what he wanted to present and he took a great deal of personal interest in that aspect of the bank.'

In attracting customers, Abedi seemed to be applying the best marketing practice, and it worked. Customers always commented on the comfort of the branch, the speed and politeness of service and so on, as compared with local banks. The Abedi philosophy of management was quite different and much less conventional. He was not content just with simple, worthy Islamic qualities, but sought to import some of the more esoteric, quasi-Sufi islamic principles into the bank's culture. This met with widespread scepticism. What, for example, did the staff make of his philosophy of the 'joint personality', a concept alleged to aid delegation? The theory here was that Abedi's most senior associates thought so alike that they acted as one and there was no need to refer back to head office. The reality was that Abedi never did anything without referring to Naqvi. But Abedi used the joint personality theory to persuade the sheikhs who liked to deal with him personally, that they should not worry if he was not there in person because the manager and he had a joint personality, and whatever the manager decided was all right with him. This was a perfect way for Abedi to put himself about, but equally it enabled managers to have quite extraordinary freedom of action, which they went on to abuse liberally. Inevitably, eyebrows were raised. 'It was not understood. There was cynicism within the organisation about joint personalities because human beings are what they are,' said Nadir Rahim.

The Muslim management style even had its own management consultants to hone it. A team of management consultants, Forum Inc, worked closely with BCCI, and Forum managing director Tom Thiss would travel to conferences such as one held in Dubai and expound on the Abedi theory of management. His firm's study of BCCI compared what BCCI called its Real Management with more traditional practices. In the BCCI column there was a separate heading:

> Major Purpose: Believes that purpose energises behaviour by engaging spirit. Gives meaning to existence (process of life) by lifting it above routine of daily activity. Ennobles effort by freeing a person from becoming the instrument of another's will. Has four-fold stated purpose.
> a) Submission to God
> b) Service to Mankind
> c) Success
> d) Giving

In the traditional style of management column there was something more recognisable:

> Does not generally have an equivalent to the BCC Major Purpose. Some organisations have a few general principles which state that they want to excel in a given field. Others have a value system that gives rise to a central thrust for quality, marketing, or product innovation. Many others talk of making a profit, satisfying the stockholders, meeting the needs of their customers, and providing a high quality of work life for their employees.

Perhaps the Abedi management style reached its apogee of egoism and obscurantism at the BCCI annual conference. The theme discussed by the entire management staff in Geneva in February 1982 was 'Submission to God, Service to Humanity, Giving and Success'. Abedi told the assembled management that his bank, BCCI, would be different; it would be charitable, it would be sympathetic to the concerns of the poor and deprived.

So successful was the discussion in Switzerland that it was followed up in March with another gathering at the Inn on the Park in London. Less than a fortnight later Abedi wrote to all his staff saying: 'As BCCI has always endeavoured to care for your spiritual and psychological needs, no less than your material requirements, it has been decided to implement the theme of '82 by initiating the process of giving. You will be paid 2½ per cent of your present salary for the year on 8 April for giving to any individual or cause in fulfilment of your instinct and good judgement.'

It was not just a one-off stunt. Abedi continued the theme, writing to 'all members of the BCCI family': 'It is in the medium of Giving that life flows into life, and God's divinity in all its embracing fullness, shines and rains softly, smoothly and blissfully on His creation.'

At BCCI conferences the previous year's balance-sheet was given just the briefest of mentions, the real object of the exercise being to instil in those attending the importance of 'moving to the spirit of God'. While speaking of humility, Abedi's gentle domination of these get-togethers was total. Recordings show that he did most of the talking while the delegates listened in spell-bound silence.

All the key players in the BCCI story attended and they spoke with a religious fervour about such weighty matters as the psyche and spirit of the bank, and the moral and philosophical dimensions of management.

Speakers were invited forward to talk when the spirit moved them, with Abedi assuring them that it was not a performance, no one cared whether they spoke well or badly. And every speaker would not only defer to Abedi himself but would heap praise on the eloquence and wisdom of the previous speaker, while apologising for his own inadequacies. Some broke down: 'Sir, I am totally overwhelmed by the proceedings of the conference,' said Khalid Imran, choking with emotion. 'After seeing these tears in your eyes, I always have these tears of gratitude. In my moments of silence, I cry that I have been associated with BCCI. Agha Sahib, I am totally overwhelmed. I may sound incoherent but I would like to say only one thing. I can do anything for this group, this family.' When the next delegate was invited forward he too was overcome by the atmosphere of the moment: 'Agha Sahib, frankly I don't find myself equal to it today.'

Conferences were always held in the most stunning surroundings. The 1984 Vienna conference was no exception, with hundreds of BCCI executives and employees along with accountants, shareholders and representatives from other banking affiliates crowding into the magnificent Hoffburg Palace. Tape-recordings of the entire event show how easily Abedi's family, as he liked to call all associated with BCCI, were swept along. From time to time Abedi would ask senior and junior employees if they felt ready to speak. When they did, it would always be to repeat Abedi's message, often with long, apologetic interruptions from Abedi himself as he tried to clarify some point. Abedi's tone was hypnotic. He would tell the audience that he wanted to reveal the truth to them. Speaking without notes, he set the tone for the conference with a lengthy speech about humility. He told his audience that BCCI's achievements would not have been so outstanding 'without the support of so many'.

There was special praise, for example, for the Abu Dhabi shareholders represented by Ghanim al-Mazrui. 'But for their financial support and, more than that, for the support they have provided through their kindness and by lending us all their influence and prestige, we would not have been what we are and we would not have been sitting here as we are.' Every sentence and every phrase was interspersed with long pauses sometimes lasting nearly a minute. There was gratitude, too, for the auditors as, with terrible irony, Abedi lavished praise on their work: 'Our auditors but for whose honest and sincere appraisal of the affairs of our bank we wouldn't have got the authenticity that we have today.'

He summed up his thanks to all with these words: 'Today I am sitting before God and before you all like a child so fearful and so fondly hopeful of the purpose for which we have assembled, for the achievement of the purpose for which we have assembled. I feel so humble and so respectful to you. And I am hoping that during these two days we would have moments when all of us will feel humility in its true sense and in its true value in the same moment,' he warbled repetitively.

Not all were carried away by the mood. Abedi's lengthy monologues sent some of the more elderly directors to sleep, as the talking continued into the small hours. Some of the American visitors tried to catch the theme but, as one representative from the National Bank of Georgia demonstrated, not all had Abedi's gift of speech, and he was driven to talk about hard facts and figures: 'I feel totally engulfed at times in the feelings I have for my colleagues and for you [BCCI] as well. I was most impressed by your profit numbers and your growth since the beginning.'

The catering staff of the Hoffburg Palace were certainly not 'engulfed' by Abedi's cavalier attitude to the timetable. On several occasions he skipped the planned tea-break because he did not want to 'break the mood' of the moment. The mood of the catering manager was such that BCCI was asked not to return if it planned to continue that way.

The group also preached some of the principles of Islamic banking. The practice of course was quite different. The teaching of the Koran prohibits Muslims from earning interest or *riba*, a rule which started causing significant problems as the oil boom began producing untold wealth in petrodollars. So a way had to be found for the bank to get round the difficulty and still operate in the financial markets of the world.

The Saudis solved the problem neatly, simply by calling interest profit. General Zia, a strict Muslim – or so he wanted the religious leaders, the *mullahs*, to believe, for their support was important to him – sent representatives to find out how Pakistan could benefit from Islamic banking. One of their first ports of call was M. R. Pirbhai, an old friend from Habib Bank days who regularly gave legal advice to Abedi. Puzzled by their motives, he would give a wry smile and advise them to look no further than Saudi Arabia. There, he said, they simply called interest profit. If they wanted something more sophisticated, they could undertake Murabaha transactions. Under this system an investor lends his money to a bank. The bank agrees to buy goods which a third party will produce using the lender's money to buy raw materials. The bank agrees to buy at a premium usually fixed to prevailing interest rates. The profit is made when the goods are sold. The risk is that the company will fail and be unable to pay back the loan, so a letter of credit is often given by another bank, for which the producing company pays a fee.

This form of Islamic banking showed a remarkable growth during the early 1980s. In 1984 BCCI simply developed their own twist on the system when they set up their own Islamic Banking Unit in London; it was here that the most serious false accounting is said to have taken place. BCCI did not go to a second bank for a letter of credit but simply issued its own, thereby exposing it to bear the whole risk if the company went bust. At its peak, towards the end of 1989, Islamic customers had placed $1.4 billion with BCCI.

Traditional bankers frowned on Islamic banking practices generally – funds produced through Islamic banking are not considered to be genuine deposits under the Banking Act. As far as the regulators are concerned, the transaction is asset management by another name and should be kept separate. Officially the depositors are taking too great a risk as they are so dependent on the success of the producer. In the case of BCCI, depositors were completely unaware that their money was being placed elsewhere within the BCCI group or on the money markets.

In their report of 22 June 1991, BCCI's auditors, Price Waterhouse, wrote: 'The resulting catalogue of errors with regard to the non-repayment of some placements and the misuse of other placements as security reflects at the very least a lack of any proper independent management control in the UK region.' The irony was that M. R. Pirbhai advised his visitors from Pakistan against getting involved in Islamic banking but he was overruled . . . by the Bank of England who gave BCCI permission to start operating it.

Fundamental to the BCCI philosophy as expressed by Abedi was the charitable purpose, the Giving. As usual, he imported lawyers to find him a tax-efficient company web, even while he was planning good works. In September 1981 Abedi established the Cayman-based BCCI Foundation which was to be funded from BCCI Holdings in Luxembourg through BCCI Pakistan. The good causes it supported were well publicised. For example, there was the work in the Orangi Project in one of Karachi's worst slums, where millions of rupees went into improving facilities, both medical and basic.

It cannot have been accidental that the offshore connection was highly tax-efficient. The Foundation enjoyed a special tax-free status in Pakistan, and within two years of its inauguration it had received nearly 1½ billion rupees of untaxed profits from BCCI's activities in the country. But BCCI's special tax status had to be earned. One of the biggest single beneficiaries of the Foundation's largesse was the Society for the Promotion of Engineering Sciences and Technology. The bulk of that money eventually found its way to the Ghulam Ishaq Khan Institute for Engineering, Sciences and Technology. The Institute is named after the President of Pakistan, who as finance minister approved the tax-free position of the BCCI Foundation.

At the top of the family tree in the Cayman Islands was ICIC Apex Holdings. It was described as a charity, but to all intents and purposes it was non-operational. Further down the tree was the ICIC Foundation's London office and the BCCI head office which was the conduit for funds from BCCI Holdings in Luxembourg. From that sprang the Third World Foundation.

If charity was Abedi's real motivation, then he was hopelessly let down by the people he gathered around him. A classic example of the shenanigans of his associates was the running of the Third World Foundation, the Third World Group and its satellite companies which involved the larger-than-life figure of Altaf Gauhar.

Gauhar, a long-time friend of Abedi from his early Pakistan days, is immensely well connected. He was secretary to the government in the days of Ayub Khan, and according to those who know him best, he was Khan's 'conscience keeper'. Gauhar is reputed to have ghosted Khan's autobiography. Nadir Rahim describes Gauhar as a 'remarkable mind, an academe'. While conceding that Gauhar might have 'run amok', he states that at the time he was regarded as a 'very powerful and seasoned civil servant'.

When Bhutto came to power Gauhar lost favour. Charges were levelled against him and he was arrested. The incestuous bonds which seem to draw everyone into Abedi's web took an exotic twist during Gauhar's trial. It turned out that Raqaya Kabir, sister of Abedi's chief financial officer, Masihur Rahman, admitted that she was Gauhar's mistress. Raqaya and another of her brothers worked for Gauhar in a subsidiary of the Third World Group's operations called Interspace Communications UK. Despite the fancy title it sold clothes – it was in the rag trade.

Gauhar was well attuned to Abedi's predilection for helping the less fortunate and suggested that a Third World Foundation should be established, but again the control from the centre was to be remarkably lax. Gauhar recommended that there should be three trustees: Abedi, Naqvi and himself. But because Abedi and Naqvi had such great commitments elsewhere, it was written into the constitution that they would have no responsibility for the actions and decisions of Gauhar who was also the secretary-general. Abedi and Naqvi went along with the suggestion, saying from the start that they would be much too busy to get involved.

Disaffected colleagues said that 'whenever Gauhar found it convenient he took money from the Third World Foundation and put it into South Publications'. South Publications' magazine, *South*, frequently published eloquent contributions from Gauhar himself before it was finally wound up in 1990. Gauhar's son, Humayun, also worked for South Publications, and again according to one board member, 'Father and son drew large salaries. South Publications were continuously running at a loss. What they were doing was just putting expenses down to charity.'

BCCI donated $10 million to the Third World Foundation and much of it was squandered on lavish conferences in exotic locations like Manila and China. Friends, families and their servants as well as world leaders and journalists were all put up at the finest hotels, all expenses paid. The gatherings were always well attended. Ted Heath, the former British prime minister, was a guest at the Manila conference.

Another worthy cause which Gauhar invented was the Third World prize. He persuaded Abedi that it could match the Nobel Prize in prestige. The Prize, like so much of Abedi's charitable work, looked ethical to those on the outside, but was in fact totally self-serving.

There was the loftiness of the ideal – a prize awarded to people who had contributed most to the Third World, with the backing of such figures as Javier Perez de Cuellar, Secretary-General of the United Nations, and Indira Gandhi, former Prime Minister of India. The list of recipients of the $100,000 prize reflects BCCI's drive for international recognition, although as far as Abedi and his self-interest were concerned, who gave and who received probably did not matter, and sometimes, the giver was much more important to Abedi than the recipient.

1980 Dr Paul Prebish, international development economist from Argentina, with Dr Kurt Waldheim, the UN Secretary-General in attendance.

1981 Dr Julius Nyerere, President of Tanzania, was presented with the prize by Indira Gandhi, Prime Minister of India.

1982 Zhao Ziyang, the Chinese premier, in a colourful ceremony in Beijing presented the prize to the International Rice Research Institute of Manila.

1983 Professor Arvid Pardo, the Maltese UN diplomat, received his prize from Belisario Betancur, President of Colombia.

1984 Willy Brandt, former German chancellor, with the new UN Secretary-General, Javier Perez de Cuellar, giving his approval.

1985 Nelson and Winnie Mandela. The prize was received on their behalf by Oliver Tambo of the African National Congress from the Prime Minister of Malaysia, Dr Mahathir Mohammad.

1986 Bob Geldof, for his work in raising funds for Ethiopia.
1987 The International Planned Parenthood Federation of India received the prize from the President of Brazil, Jose Sarney.
1988 Gro Harlem Brundtland, the Norwegian Prime Minister, presented by Robert Mugabe, Prime Minister of Zimbabwe.

But all the time, Abedi was buying influence. The Charity Commission was not impressed by his motives and refused to grant the Third World Prize charitable status. Abedi turned to a Cayman Island company to acquire a tax break on the Prize. How much money went into genuine charitable causes was always disputed. A source on the ICIC (International Credit and Investment Company) Foundation board said that Gauhar established a company before the Trust was set up, and the $10 million from BCCI went first into that company of which he and his son were directors: 'One fine morning he [Gauhar] drew $7,200,000 and put it in his personal account in London. When I came to know about it I told him he should immediately refund the money otherwise I would take action. So he refunded $7 million but not the $200,000 he said he had spent on work for the Prize. Until this day he has not returned the $200,000.' The trustees then informed the Charity Commission about these unusual transactions and suggested it should look more closely at some of the lavish apartments being maintained by Gauhar and his son in London.

It was not all cynical manipulation and self-interest, however. The bank helped to finance the education of some of the brightest children in the Third World who could not afford to achieve better academic qualifications. BCCI was a major contributor to Cambridge University's Commonwealth Trust to which Abedi had been introduced by Lord Callaghan in 1982. Abedi was on the board of trustees along with Lord Callaghan, Dr Kenneth Kaunda and Sir Shridath Ramphal under the chairmanship of the Prince of Wales. The bank's contributions have enabled BCCI Cambridge scholars from Pakistan, India, Bangladesh, Sri Lanka, Zambia, Zimbabwe and China to attend the University. Abedi and Callaghan even travelled to Zimbabwe one summer to inaugurate the Zimbabwe Cambridge Trust.

But even then there was a taint. Opposition MPs in the Pakistan Parliament said that more than fifty of the scholars who had been assisted by BCCI were sons and daughters of politicians. The bank's defence to that charge, however, is that it was inevitable that the students with the qualifications would come from better-off homes.

BCCI had one other important area of influence in the charitable world. It was a major sponsor of Global 2000, a private organisation devoted to promoting self-sufficiency in the Third World by raising health standards and improving the environment. The driving force behind the project was former US President Jimmy Carter, who first met Abedi in the early 1980s when Abedi visited Carter's home in Georgia. That meeting was followed up by a series of trips to countries throughout Africa and Asia, and culminated in contributions worth $8 million from the bank. Abedi became co-chairman of the organisation. It may be no accident that at this time Carter's former associate Bert Lance was pushing through Abedi's acquisition of First

American under the noses of the US Federal regulators.

When news of the bank's closure was announced, Carter said he was 'shocked and disturbed'. At the time he had checked with the Justice Department and had accepted their assurances about BCCI. 'We didn't know the facts. I don't know how much of the facts was known by anybody in this country,' said Carter. Carter was not alone in having BCCI wool pulled over his eyes. Many who liked to believe that protestations of ethics and generosity were genuine were to be similarly duped.

# 4 The Duping of the Shah

In the 1970s Abedi was desperate for Muslim funds, and looked jealously on the legendary wealth of the Shah of Persia. The schemes he used to access that wealth mirror his subsequent assault on Financial General in the United States. They show that from the very start of BCCI, Abedi was determined that his insatiable ambition would not be stopped by local laws barring foreign investors, and that he was already prepared to use schemes to buy nominee shareholdings with bribes and other favours.

Links between Iran and Pakistan had traditionally been close; both countries were Muslim and both were members of the Regional Cooperation and Development group. Iran was also the land of Abedi's ancestors, which may have had a symbolic significance.

Connections between the high-flying Pakistani and Iran date back to 1970, two years before he founded BCCI. Abedi was looking for a partner in Iran, and he had heard on the narrow Pakistani grapevine that a rival bank, Habib, had approached a lawyer and wealthy owner of an insurance company in Tehran, Dr Ali Reza Saheb. Saheb, a former assistant to Mohammed Mossadeq, the Iranian populist leader in the twenties, was well connected in political, financial and royal circles and would provide an excellent introduction. Saheb had entertained executives of Habib in Tehran but turned down their approach. Abedi thought he would try his luck along the same route.

He offered to fly Saheb over to London, and the two men met in Abedi's palatial suite at the Hilton on Park Lane. It was the start of a process of blandishment which lasted for the best part of a decade. Saheb had dreamt of making Tehran a money centre for the region which would attract both Gulf money and American banking business, and Abedi seemed to share some of the same aspirations. He could already boast having made good contacts among Gulf rulers as well as tentative steps into American banking.

The two men met again in Tehran, when Abedi was accompanied by Swaleh Naqvi and two other close colleagues from United Bank, Dildar Rezvi and Velayat Hussein Abedi. This time there was something more concrete on the table. An Iranian private bank, Asnaaf Bank, had collapsed, and the local authorities were looking for a rescue; Saheb saw a joint venture between Abedi's United Bank and the collapsed bank as the vehicle.

There began a period of negotiations between the two groups. Abedi's hospitality and spending power were formidable. Ali Reza Saheb remembers one negotiation in Zurich when his wife and Abedi's newly married second wife, the air hostess Rabia, went on a spending spree on a Saturday. Money was no limit, but the two women ran out of cash, so Abedi told Naqvi to find the treasurer of the United Bank's branch in Zurich who opened the safe and took out the cash.

Abedi successfully completed negotiations and United Bank was allotted a 40 per cent holding in the joint venture, the maximum amount of shares that Iranian law permitted to a foreign bank; the Iranian partner kept the remainder.

The joint venture appears to have been effected without the knowledge of the Pakistani Prime Minister, Zulfiqar Ali Bhutto. When Bhutto heard about it in the course of a visit to Tehran, he publicly berated his ambassador, saying, 'Abedi is not a straightforward man. He will be out of control.' The Pakistani Prime Minister was also concerned that the joint venture would spoil his hopes for building a relationship between Pakistan and Iran. Bhutto later heard that Abedi had set up BCCI which was registered outside Pakistan, in Luxembourg, and he made him *persona non grata* in Pakistan and withdrew his passport. Bhutto was convinced that Abedi had acquired the funds to set up BCCI by making improper loans to his friends, and shortly afterwards he nationalised Pakistan's banks.

Saheb already had some reservations about working with Abedi. At one stage the Pakistani had promised the Iranian a 25 per cent stake in BCCI in return for his holding in the newly formed bank. In fact Abedi never came up with the shares, but he told Saheb that 'it was his bank and he could have shares in it whenever he wanted'.

The nationalisation of the Pakistani banks meant that the Iranian venture had to cease, but Saheb and Abedi continued to do business together. The dream of a joint Iranian and Pakistani bank persisted, and this time Saheb went to Abedi for help. Saheb planned to allot wealthy Arab sheikhs 35 per cent of the shares in a new bank and needed introductions. Abedi went one better; he gave him a list of willing shareholders but said he would like BCCI to have 17 per cent of the shares, and the Arab investors 18 per cent.

Abedi's list included Sheikh Zayed of Abu Dhabi and his son, Sheikh Khalifa, the Sultan of Sharjah, Sheikh Qabus of Oman and Sheikh Rashid of Dubai. The list was cleared by the Iranian security service, and the shareholdings of the new bank seemed assured. But then Abedi introduced a last-minute hitch. He told Saheb, who was to be the new bank's deputy chairman, that 'Unless someone from the Iranian royalty became a shareholder, the participation of the Arabs was in danger'. This surprised the Iranians, since the issue had not arisen before, but Saheb went to the head of Iranian Central Bank, who in turn went to the Shah, and the latter eventually cleared his brother, Prince Mahmood Reza Pahlavi, to join the board of the newly formed Iran/Arab Bank.

Abedi and Naqvi, who were staying in Tehran at the time keeping a watchful eye on the proceedings, insisted on visiting Prince Mahmood, and within ten minutes were in the Prince's office. Says Saheb, 'They talked to him as if they were talking to a god. They made themselves subservient, bowing profusely. Then Abedi said to the Prince, "Your Highness, we would like to present you with 2,000 shares in Bank of Credit and Commerce." The Prince asked Abedi, "How much do I have to pay?" but Abedi and Naqvi said, "This is your bank, don't worry, we'll arrange it."'

Several years later, in 1976, Saheb asked Sheikh Hamdan of Abu Dhabi (the father of the current ruler) about the unexpected request by the Arab shareholders for a member of the royal family to sit on the bank's board. The Sheikh said this had never happened, and he put it down to 'one of Abedi's tricks. Sheikh Zayed and myself don't like the Shah,' he said, 'he's too arrogant for us. We sit on the floor and eat without servants, not in palaces like him.' Hamdan told Saheb how Abedi frequently came to see the Gulf sheikhs with projects and would wait around their palaces for hours, buttonholing anyone who would speak to him and becoming a figure of fun in the process. But sometimes, said Hamdan, the sheikhs would accede to his requests 'just to get rid of him'.

The Shah's brother, Prince Mahmood, had now become part of the BCCI circle of big Arab names. When Abedi furnished the UK banking magazine *Euromoney* with the list of BCCI shareholders in 1978, the Prince was named as the 'Iranian royal family', to the dismay of the Shah who knew nothing about the shares.

BCCI gave their new royal Iranian investor the Persian carpet treatment for the next five years, and then pulled the rug firmly from under his feet. To begin with, he was allowed to borrow $200,000 to acquire a penthouse in Belgravia, furnished at BCCI's expense. Whenever Prince Mahmood was in London he was attended by Abedi's assistant at the time, Dildar Rezvi, who took him shopping to buy shirts and ties in Jermyn Street, and also organised all his hotel accommodation and travel.

Then came the Iranian revolution, and BCCI's open-handed generosity turned into a tight fist. The squeeze on Prince Mahmood was in two stages. First, Saheb, who had been given power of attorney over Mahmood's financial affairs, recalls that late in 1978, when the crowds were on the streets of Tehran baying for the Shah's blood, Velayat Hussein Abedi, Agha Hasan Abedi's loyal assistant, came to him and told him that BCCI would like the Prince's account to be cleared. Saheb asked what he owed, and he was told the Prince owed the bank for the price of the BCCI shares and the cost of antiques the bank had bought for his flat, a total bill of $350,000. The Prince agreed to sell his London penthouse.

The *coup de grâce* came when Naqvi and V. H.

Abedi went to see Prince Mahmood while he was a fugitive from Iran in Morocco and highly demoralised. They delivered the customary large bouquet of flowers and then told him that it was 'no longer in your interest or ours for you to remain a shareholder in BCCI. You don't want the Iranian government to accuse you of swindling millions of Iranian money to buy BCCI shares,' they threatened, 'so it's better we keep the shares in trust for you. We will transfer the shares to our accounts, but you can trust us to look after you.' At the same time BCCI offered to pay the Prince a $6,000 monthly dividend on the shares, and Mahmood agreed to the deal.

After twelve instalments the payments stopped, and the Prince went to Saheb and asked for his help. Saheb approached Naqvi who said that 'BCCI's sources in other banks' disclosed that the Prince had $4.5 million in Citibank in New York, and he should not worry about it. Saheb was powerless, and a deeply resentful Prince Mahmood, who now lives in California, is planning to sue BCCI for the value of his misappropriated shares and other funds.

Saheb's treatment at the hands of BCCI shareholders was no more friendly. Once the bank was founded they did all they could to undermine him with a share-buying campaign. Saheb quickly learned that Abedi voted all the Arab sheikhs' shares as if they were part of the BCCI block, and all the money owed by the sheikhs for their initial share purchases came from BCCI.

Then it became clear that the BCCI shareholders were not content just to have 35 per cent, and they started to increase their shares. Iranian law allowed a non-Iranian up to 40 per cent of an Iranian bank, but Abedi was pushing 40 per cent and still was not stopping. He had detailed Velayat Hussein Abedi (who was later to head up the London operation) to contact Iranians, and he began buying shares in the bank using the names of sympathetic Iranians who would vote the shares for BCCI. V. H. Abedi had some formal documentation drawn up outlining how the nominees would keep half the shares for themselves, and the other half would go into a secret BCCI nominee account.

One of the primary participants in the share-buying scheme for the Iran/Arab Bank was Rahim Irvani, an Iranian acquaintance of Saheb's, who had established a major business manufacturing shoes for export. Saheb invited Irvani to subscribe for 1 per cent of the shares at the outset, but Irvani using his Alvand Investment company quickly increased his holding to 6 per cent. He did this by buying those shares allotted to the bank's managing director, Cyrus Samii, who it was later revealed had accepted payments from BCCI.

Irvani struck up a close social as well as business relationship with Abedi over the years, entertaining him whenever he came to Tehran. Irvani later served as a BCCI nominee director on the board of Credit and Commerce American Holdings (CCAH), the BCCI company used to disguise its control over First American Bank. Abedi repaid Irvani for this and other favours by extending to him loans worth tens of millions of dollars to set up shoe-manufacturing plants in Cairo and Atlanta, Georgia. Many of these were non-performing, according to a BCCI officer.

Irvani was at the centre of Abedi's Iranian circle of contacts. He introduced Abedi to James Helms, the American ambassador to Iran and a former CIA chief in the United States, and may also have employed Roy

Carlson, a former Bank of America officer in Abu Dhabi. Carlson moved over to BCCI to work with Naqvi in Abu Dhabi and subsequently headed up the newly acquired National Bank of Georgia for BCCI.

As well as trying to increase his shareholding in Iran/Arab Bank, Abedi also seconded BCCI employees to Tehran to influence day-to-day management. The first was Iqbal Rezvi whom BCCI set up in considerable style in Tehran. He joined the bank as a consultant to the managing director, but the board refused him an executive role, and he left within six months. Then Abedi introduced Azizullah Choudry, a banker from his close circle. Choudry stayed longer but never moved out of the credit department.

BCCI ensured that its Gulf shareholders and their families were properly looked after when they passed through Tehran. On one occasion in the mid-1970s, Sheikh Hamdan, a BCCI shareholder, was due to visit Tehran, and Abedi asked Saheb to provide cars and a driver. Saheb also had a dinner appointment with the Sheikh, but the venue was changed from a restaurant to the Sheikh's hotel suite. When Saheb arrived, he asked one of the Sheikh's companions if the arrangements were working out all right. He was told that 'the Sheikh is taken care of'. Saheb went into the lounge and discovered 'four or five of the prettiest girls I have seen in my life serving the guests wine. They were very young and some came from Morocco and only spoke Arabic.' Saheb made his apologies and left, but he suspected the hand of Savak, the Shah's internal security service, since the foreign girls would have needed permission to enter the country. Later Saheb heard from a Pakistani minister that Abedi was the source of this entertainment.

Abedi skilfully left Saheb guessing about his intentions towards him. One one occasion he even suggested to Saheb that he might like to be a nominee for BCCI which he explained was trying to buy a bank in the United States where there was a 5 per cent limitation for purchases by any one individual. Saheb says he flatly refused.

In October 1978, in London, Abedi introduced Saheb to the lawyer Clark Clifford and the banker Bert Lance, who had the ear of President Carter and were already acting for Abedi. The four men met at the Inn on the Park for lunch and the subject of the conversation was Iranian politics. Abedi appeared to be trying to impress Clifford with his worldwide high-level contacts and he introduced Saheb as an influential businessman who could bring Clifford up to date with the latest news about his country. Clifford had a number of meetings with the Iranian who wanted him to persuade President Carter to keep out of Iran. Saheb visited Washington in January 1979, where Clifford told him that the President had given an undertaking to the Shah that the Americans would support the newly appointed Prime Minister Shahpour Bakhtiar for three months. Saheb is convinced that the conversations 'went up as far as Jimmy Carter', but his pleadings had no effect. Within a month the Shah was toppled and Saheb was thrown into jail by the *mullahs*, who suspected his connections with the Americans and the Shah.

Like the Shah's brother, Prince Mahmood, Saheb would soon be given the BCCI treatment. In 1981 he was released from imprisonment in Iran and went to Pakistan, where he was entertained by Abedi. Again, Saheb was warmly welcomed as his eternal brother. Saheb discussed his finances with Abedi and explained that his businesses had money outstanding in Iran, which was frozen following the revolution. As soon as it was released, he would repay his debt.

As a token of good faith, Saheb said he would not touch $1.3 million of his personal money which he had deposited in BCCI in London, and Abedi reciprocated by saying he would pay him a monthly fee of $6,000. In 1989 Saheb wanted to access the $1.3 million following legal advice that there was no connection between his business accounts still locked in Iran and his personal money. However, he was told by the bank that the money had gone to Grand Cayman and was no longer accessible. A letter from BCCI's legal department, signed by A. M. Haidermota, legal consultant, and Saleem Malik, legal adviser, stated in no uncertain terms: 'We find your allegations and claims to be false, frivolous and wholly unjustified, and it appears that you are trying to make unconscionable gain at the expense of the bank. . . . We have been instructed by the Management not to advert to the contents of your letters under reference as they are false, and/or frivolous and/or extraneous, and are motivated to harass. Kindly therefore refrain from communicating with the Bank or with us, as no further correspondence shall be entertained on matters raised by you.' Some reward for a man once fêted by the bank's president as a 'brother', and who had given so much of himself to the bank.

# 5 US Cover-up

BCCI started as the most secret bank in the United States – so secret that the banking regulators would not allow it to show its face. That is why it used many subterfuges to disguise its presence. By the end of its stay in the USA, BCCI was the most visible bank, the subject of many congressional and senate inquiries, law enforcement investigations and media inquiries and exposures. It was a national celebrity.

The tale of BCCI in the United States falls into two distinct chapters. The first concerns the takeover of a number of banks. The second covers the laundering of drugs money.

The takeover of the largest of the banks acquired by BCCI, Financial General Bancshares Inc., which later became First American Bank, reveals a deviousness on the part of BCCI and a laxness in regulation only matched by the zeal currently displayed by American supervisors and public investigators who are now keen to right earlier wrongs.

In 1977 Agha Hasan Abedi's dream of a world-size bank looked a long way off fulfilment. His empire had reached little further than London and the Gulf and was not making much progress in either area. Things were also going painfully slowly in Iran. Within ten years, however, BCCI boasted of controlling banks with total assets estimated at £7 billion.

Abedi and the Arab investors whom he was advising, like Kamal Adham and the Ruler of Dubai, had been casting envious glances for some time at the wealthy and (at that time) dominant American banking scene. Abedi had sent out an envoy, Abdul Sami, who regularly ran up against questions from bank supervisors about BCCI shareholders. Sami did not want to disclose information, and the Americans got suspicious. They had had a nibble at one American bank, the Bank of Commerce in New York, but BCCI pulled out at the last moment because Abedi decided that he could acquire Bank of Commerce's parent for little more than he would have to pay for this subsidiary. This was the start of BCCI's assault on Financial General, which listed among its subsidiaries banks in a number of states on the East Coast of the United States.

The fifty-year-old Washington, DC-based bank holding company was unique in the US banking system because it was not subject to the US law which prohibited a bank from owning another bank outside its home state. Financial General was represented in Washington DC, Maryland, New York, Tennessee and Virginia, and this created the opportunity for purchasers of a bank to slip between the banking codes and regulations applicable in each state. With so many state regulators involved, there might also be inefficiencies in their supervision.

On 9 November 1977 Sami and Abedi were introduced by Senator Eugene Hollis to a man who was in severe financial difficulties, and who had shares in a bank connected to Financial General, which he was ready to sell. BCCI was prepared to offer twice the going rate for the stock.

Bertram Lance was in disgrace and desperate. In September 1977 he had been forced to leave the Carter administration following a scandal over his personal finances, and this had eaten away at his one-time considerable personal wealth. Lance, who had had a successful career as a banker, had arranged the buy-out of the National Bank of Georgia (NBG) from Financial General, and personally owned 12 per cent of the shares in NBG.

Abedi and Sami were not just interested in Lance for his shares; they also liked the political connections he retained, despite his disgrace. In America more than anywhere else political power led to power in the financial system, BCCI's ultimate goal. The government post from which Lance resigned was highly prestigious. He had been director of the Office of Management and Budget, the equivalent perhaps of the British chancellor of the exchequer, and had been given the job as a reward for long service to President Jimmy Carter. Both men were from Georgia and Lance had backed Carter when he first campaigned for governor at the beginning of the 1970s and later when he ran successfully for president. He had also helped to run the finances of the State of Georgia for Carter. Lance knew the power of money – he had ensured that NBG became the single largest lender to Carter's peanut farm.

Before Sami's lunch with Lance, memos had passed between Sami and Abedi indicating that they were aware that BCCI could not front the acquisition of NBG in its own name. Georgia's State regulators would certainly want to inquire into its ownership group and the origins of the funds going towards the share purchases. The BCCI men would resist such inquiries fiercely. To avoid problems of this kind, they organised a nominee of BCCI to front the share purchase.

Abedi's front man for the NBG acquisition was Ghaith Pharaon, a Saudi who had made his home in the United States and was to prove an important BCCI investor and name there. Pharaon was a very appropriate front for the State bankers. Smooth, articulate and educated, he had mixed in high circles from an early age. The son of a Saudi doctor, he had come to the USA in 1959 to study mining. In 1965 he took a master's degree in business administration from Harvard (of which he later became the only Muslim board member) and then set up in business in Saudi Arabia. NBG was only his first enterprise for BCCI in the United States. He went on to front the purchase of other financial institutions, like the Central Bank of Independence in California in 1985, and a Savings and Loan in Miami called CenTrust which subsequently went bust.

At this stage Pharaon was still building up his portfolio, and BCCI was prepared to back him. Within a year he had arranged the entire purchase of NBG. He himself bought half the NBG shares and half were paid for by BCCI, but he acted as their nominee. Pharaon could not lose on the transaction as far as his own shares were concerned since he had been given an indemnity or 'memorandum of deposit' by BCCI.

In the mid-1980s Pharaon, by then an apparent high-flyer, got into difficulties in the United States. He had built up a portfolio of business interests like his Attock Oil and Attock Cement companies in the UK and Pakistan through BCCI, and major property and shares stakes through a Georgia-based company called Inter-Redec, but some bad deals in Argentina and Romania were pulling him down. Having helped out Agha Hasan Abedi by acting as BCCI's nominee in the United States, he now called in the debt. Abedi bailed him out of NBG, paying some 25 per cent more than the market value for his holding. BCCI depositors would later find that their funds were used and manipulated not just to pay the high price but also apparently to buy the bank twice with the same funds.

As far as Abedi was concerned, the NBG deal worked well and it was a necessary part of his plan to acquire Financial General, NBG's erstwhile parent. Lance, who was now a paid consultant at BCCI, began to introduce Abedi to a number of dissatisfied shareholders who wanted to sell out of Financial General. These included the late Dr Armand Hammer, the chairman of Occidental Petroleum, who owned around 5 per cent, and some associates of his, who also owned 5 per cent. There was another 10 per cent on the market, and Abedi wanted to snap up the lot. But he ran into the US banking regulation which held that investors were not individually allowed to own more than 5 per cent of the shares.

Abedi quickly found four Arab supporters of BCCI, whose names could be used to front the purchases. They were Saudi security chief Kamal Adham, Faisal Saud al-Fulaij, Abdullah Dharwaish, who represented Sheikh Mohammed bin-Zayed, son of Sheikh Zayed, and at that time too young to conduct his own business, and Sheikh Sultan bin-Zayed. Abedi felt confident that the committee men who ran State banking institutions would pass these through on the nod.

The pugnacious chairman of Financial General whose company was now under assault was rather less pliable. William Middendorf, a former secretary to the Navy in the American government, lodged a complaint in March 1978 with the Securities and Exchange Commission, arguing that the four men were acting in concert. Under American law, people acting in concert may not own in total more than 5 per cent of the shares.

Bert Lance, the man who had helped Abedi out with

the acquisition of NBG and was now his man in US financial circles, came to his aid. He passed the BCCI president on to the firm of lawyers who had advised Lance at the time of his resignation from the Carter cabinet. The firm was headed by the eminent Clark Clifford and at his side was the bright up-and-coming Robert Altman, who in turn had at his side his glamorous wife Lynda Carter, TV's Wonder Woman. (The only wondering Clifford would be doing by the end of the saga was how he ever got himself mixed up in such a mess.) The questions which would be asked then would prove much tougher than anything Clifford was about to face from US bank regulators. He was embarking on a client relationship which would irrevocably smear his eminent reputation and lead to embarrassing resignations.

Abedi found Clifford a potent ally not just because of the legal expertise he could command, but also because he had many friends and clients in the highest echelon of American politics. Clifford had been the trusted adviser of Presidents Truman and Kennedy. His firm had offices in both Washington and New York, and while he moved easily on Capitol Hill, his partner Altman knew his way around Wall Street and the Securities and Exchange Commission (SEC).

The two men led BCCI's campaign in what became a bitter takeover battle for Financial General. Middendorf argued vehemently to the SEC that BCCI's connections with Bank of America precluded the purchase. BCCI's men Clifford and Altman replied that BCCI only participated as advisers to the Arab investors, not as principals.

Altman, who dealt with the details of the immediate case, is said to have told Abedi that he had committed a technical breach, but he could sort it out. Yet BCCI clearly could not be seen to be owning stock under its own name in Financial General, let alone controlling the bank. It therefore needed a parallel company which would give the appearance of independence to the regulators but would in fact be controlled by BCCI. Abedi also needed a set of investors for the new company who would give the appearance of neutrality but would in fact act on behalf of the bank and ensure its control.

Memos that passed between Sami in Washington and Abedi in Karachi not only confirm that the operation was masterminded by BCCI, but also indicate that the bank put up these individuals to bypass US regulations prohibiting an individual from acquiring more than 5 per cent of an American bank's shares without a notification to the authorities.

In one telex to Abedi on 30 January 1978, Sami warned: 'We must be careful that our name [BCCI] does not appear as financier to most of [the investors] for this acquisition.' The company he created in the summer of 1978 for this shell-game, as it was later called, was based in the highly unregulated Netherlands Antilles, and it was called Credit and Commerce American Holdings (CCAH). Companies of this kind can be bought off the shelf in almost any offshore haven, but the Netherlands Antilles had considerable appeal at this time because of a taxation treaty between the United States and the Netherlands. A second company used for the scheme, Credit and Commerce American Investments (CCAI), was based in the Cayman Islands.

Abedi's investors and BCCI's nominees were a combination of powerful Saudis and minor dignitaries in the Arab world. Trading on the influence of his patron, the Sheikh of Abu Dhabi, Abedi had trawled the Gulf and further afield for supporters who would have little idea of his purpose or methods. In this way he came across Humaid bin Rashid al-Naomi, the Ruler of Ajman, Sheikh Hamad bin Mohammed al-Sharqi, the Ruler of the Emirate of Fujairah, and Ali Mohammed Shorafa, the Director of Presidential Affairs for the United Arab Emirates. His Saudi supporters were much more canny. They included BCCI shareholder and colleague, Ghaith Pharaon, security chief Kamal Adham, Adham's assistant El-Sayed Jawhary (also called Gohary) and businessman Abdul Raouf Khalil.

Adham became by far the most controversial figure. When Adham was introduced to the regulators during these early investigations, Clark Clifford began by describing him as 'a prominent businessman in Saudi Arabia', going on to say, 'I have come to have the deepest respect for his character, for his reputation, for his honour and for his integrity.' Clifford apparently referred to Adham as 'His Excellency'. The regulators did not want to risk offending this Saudi dignitary and began to follow suit.

But Adham's reputation was rather less honourable. He had little experience of banking, but was a past master of political intrigue. Now sixty-two, Adham is the half-brother of Iffat, a wife of the late King Faisal of Saudi Arabia, and was a close confidant of the King. He was given the job of chief of the Foreign Liaison Bureau, with the responsibility of looking after Faisal's security, at a time when radical elements in the Middle East were beginning to threaten the area's autocratic barons. In Anthony Sampson's book *The Seven Sisters*, Adham is described as Faisal's 'chamberlain'.

He also acquired prestige in the shady world of the security service where ruthlessness is more highly prized than democratic instincts. When he made a visit to Iran in 1975, Adham was fêted by Savak. He also had close contacts with the CIA and sought to influence the policy of Anwar Sadat in Egypt by pushing large sums of money his way to encourage him to expel Soviet advisers. He is understood to have been behind Saudi Arabia's policy of backing the PLO in the mid-1970s.

In addition to running the country's internal security, Adham became a major force in organising Saudi Arabia's external security resources. As early as the mid-1960s, Adham was representing some of the world's largest arms companies, and at the end of the decade he was the intermediary for Saudi Arabia in arranging for the purchase of French weapons by Egypt. Later he represented Boeing; in the mid-1970s US government agencies investigated 'questionable payments' following a massive aircraft sale to Egypt.

The regulators were bemused by the proposals for the new company with its purportedly independent investors. They held numerous hearings with Clifford, Altman and, on one occasion, with Kamal Adham and the three other investors. Adham had even been bold enough to accept the challenge apparently being thrown down by the regulators: 'It appears from the line of questions that there is suspicion that somebody from BCCI is behind all of this deal. I would like to assure you that each of us in his own right will not accept in any way to be a cover for somebody else. . . . We don't need anybody to use us, to be a cover for them. We are doing it for ourselves.' Apparently satisfied, the regulators eventually allowed the new shareholders through.

Then the share-buying began in earnest. Abedi reassured the regulators that 'All of the investors in CCAH have substantial funds, and the funds to be used by each of them to purchase their equity interest in CCAH will be provided from their personal funds.' It later emerged that they were funded by BCCI.

In a written reply to the Federal Board's questions about the relationship between BCCI and CCAH, Altman felt confident enough to answer: 'With regard to the stockholders of CCAH, all holdings constitute personal investments. None is held as an unidentified agent for another individual or organisation.'

BCCI controlled about a quarter of CCAH's shares from day one, and steadily built up a majority holding. In April 1982 CCAH and CCAI (Credit and Commerce American Investment) acquired all the shares in Financial General and in August they renamed the company First American Bancshares.

There were some 'new' names on the board to give the regulators comfort. Lawyer and political fixer Clark Clifford was made managing director of CCAH, his partner Robert Altman and a former senator and client of Clifford, Stuart Symington, became directors. Symington and Clifford who both came from Missouri, were 'Carter's men'. Like Adham and Faisal Saud al-Fulaij, Symington had a further link with the arms industry as a lobbyist for McDonnell Douglas.

The process whereby BCCI manipulated the control of the shares in CCAH, using the investors' 'names' and money to dupe the regulators about the company's independence is painstakingly documented in the Federal Reserve's document of proceedings of 29 July

1991. The trail of letters and contracts is extraordinarily complete, which raises the question of why it took almost ten years for the process to be tracked and intercepted.

The use of front men, or nominees to disguise the true ownership and control of First American, is really only the start of the First American fraud. Having given their name to BCCI, the bank proceeded to use a series of nominee companies and individuals to fabricate the bank's finances and capital structure.

The means used are described by the American congressional investigator Jack Blum. Said Blum, who later took the share-rigging to the New York investigators, and is in no doubt that the pattern of share-buying by nominees, blank share transfers and pay-offs was thoroughly corrupt, 'Many of the payments were supposed to be capital infusions into First American, that's BCCI. In fact they were loans made by other components of the same group to straw men. Any time they needed money, one unit of the bank would lend money to someone who didn't know he was borrowing it, and he in turn would wind up getting stock which in turn was pledged for a loan which was never performing.

'It's a shell-game, because you have several off-shore entities, BCCI in the Cayman, BCCI in Luxembourg, and ICIC, and they were able to lend money one to another and capitalise each other. One morning a loan would be created and you would wind up as a shareholder, just having borrowed millions of dollars. The paper would follow showing you as a shareholder and a loan where you would neither have to pay back the principal nor the interest because they would simply increase the amount of the loan as the interest increased. There was no substance in it, it was all high-flying paper.'

The Federal Reserve indictment shows how this worked. For example, in August 1982, CCAH wanted to raise money and it issued some more Financial General shares to do so. Sheikh Khalifa bin-Zayed al-Nahyan, the Crown Prince of Abu Dhabi, took Financial General shares, but the indictment shows that 'the shares were purchased with funds drawn by Swaleh Naqvi', from Khalifa's personal account at BCCI. This suggests that BCCI was paying for the shares and that the reason Khalifa was buying them was to help BCCI fill a hole in its capital. The only collateral for the loan to Khalifa which he needed to buy the shares will have been the shares themselves, indicating how BCCI involved itself in share-kiting of the kind Blum described.

Three other BCCI supporters who had already invested in Financial General, Faisal Saud al-Fulaij, Abdul Raouf Khalil and Ali Mohammed Shorafa, also bought CCAH or Financial General shares, using this little arrangement. They did not have quite the same close relationship with Naqvi as did Khalifa, and they had to take out a special loan from BCCI, or its Cayman offshoot, ICIC (Overseas), to acquire them.

The indictment lists a multitude of purchases by Adham where he borrowed money from BCCI or ICIC (Overseas), BCCI promising him each time that he would have 'no liability for any deficiency'. At the company's peak, Adham nominally controlled 16.8 per cent of CCAH shares.

Another investor, Faisal Saud al-Fulaij, seemed to negotiate an even better deal. In return for giving his name for ICIC (Overseas) investments, he would receive 25 per cent of the profits, but all the risk would be covered by ICIC (Overseas). Al-Fulaij, the chairman of Kuwait Airways, whose personal fortune has been put at $70 million, was a business associate of Adham. Al-Fulaij is thought to have teamed up with the Saudi on the Boeing deal with Egypt, and the US Federal Trade Commission has named him as the recipient of at least one bribe. Al-Fulaij had been closely associated with BCCI since its early days and from the late 1970s was chairman of its Kuwait International Finance Company (KIFCO) affiliate.

In 1985 al-Fulaij wrote to ICIC (Overseas) apparently renouncing his 25 per cent profit share. He told ICIC that they could do what they liked with his shares, and he enclosed some blank share transfer deeds in case they wanted to move the shares kept in his name to anybody else's account. Al-Fulaij received $100,000 every year between 1986 and 1989, and in 1990 he received an extra $606,000 'for his services as a nominee'. He held shares amounting to 9.1 per cent of CCAH.

In 1986 one of the more curious share-buying incidents took place. On 25 July there was another rights offering by CCAH, whereby some new shares would come on to the market so that BCCI could raise some more money. The 15,292 of the new shares were available to a company called Mashriq, which was wholly owned by Sheikh Hamad bin-Mohammed al-Sharqi, the Ruler of the Emirate of Fujairah. However, BCCI, which as ever was masterminding the share-buying, arranged for the Mashriq company to take only 8,550 of these shares, even though they were actually going for less than the market price.

The shares were not left on the market, however.

Instead, the cut-price stock was bought by the two men who were supposed to be the neutral and prestigious directors of the CCAH board, Clark Clifford and Robert Altman. Both have of course since denied that they knew that CCAH and BCCI were controlled by the same people.

Abdul Raouf Khalil, the shadowy Middle Eastern businessman thought to own a museum in Jeddah, who participated in the share-buying of CCAH and BCCI shares, received $15 million for the use of his name to purchase 5.9 per cent of the shares. Adham's assistant, El-Sayed Jawhary, received $150,000 a year for the use of his name, and another investor, Ali Mohammed Shorafa, received double that. The Mashriq Holding Company was one of the biggest names used by BCCI and at one time controlled almost 25 per cent of all the shares in CCAH.

Sheikh al-Naomi, the Ruler of the Emirate of Ajman, received the princely sum of $6.5 million for CCAH shares which he owned, although their market value may not have exceeded $4 million. However, the Ruler of Ajman was a very pliant nominee and he executed blank share certificates at Naqvi's will.

Further proof, if it were still needed, that BCCI controlled the shares held by the likes of al-Fulaij and Shorafa came in 1986 when BCCI needed new money to shore up its capital after the disaster with its treasury operation. Recapitalisation was achieved by selling both BCCI shares and the CCAH shares it controlled to a major new investor. This was the moment when the bin-Mahfouz family of Saudi Arabia which owns the Saudi National Commercial Bank came on to the CCAH books with the acquisition of $250 million worth of CCAH shares. It meant a major reshaping of the register. The family stayed only three years in CCAH, and when they quit in October 1989, their CCAH shares reverted to the original nominees, with all the existing nominees scaling up their interests.

A source close to Abedi suggests that BCCI's ownership of Financial General shares was not deliberate. He said, 'The price paid to the sellers of the stock had increased, and the people who wanted to invest in the bank did not have so much money, but they couldn't back out. So they borrowed from BCCI, and that's how the shares were placed with BCCI. When the dividends could not cover the interest on the loans, the investors' loans to BCCI were increasing. Abedi thought it would be better to agree terms whereby some of the shares would be held on BCCI's account because he thought their value would increase. He agreed terms with the investors that some of the shareholding would be theirs, and they would hold the remainder in their name, as a nominee for BCCI.'

BCCI did not simply buy and sell CCAH's shares at will, it also selected the bank's staff. For example, Aijaz Afridi, who was vice-president of First American in New York between 1983 and 1987, was a long-time employee of BCCI who had worked for the bank in Luxembourg and for its affiliate in Geneva. Abedi himself asked Afridi in 1983 if he would like the New York job; the connection between the two banks was so close that Afridi was said to have been in almost daily contact with BCCI's London office and he attended several BCCI annual conferences. He later went to head BCCI in Spain. The first president of First American was Bruno Richter who was suggested for the post by Abedi, and when Richter himself wanted to appoint members of staff they were obliged to go through interviews in London with Abedi, Afridi and Naqvi. Nor was Abedi content simply to appoint staff and let them get on with it. First American's activities were monitored closely through the Americas Coordinating Committee which Abedi had established in about 1984. The first meeting was held in New York on 24 April 1985 when Afridi took the chair and described the committee's purpose as 'coordinating the efforts of different locations of BCCI and other institutions so that the President's [Abedi's] desire to have a totality in approach is achieved'.

The acquisition of a bank using offshore shells to disguise ownership and to put the bank out of the way of regulation may be deceitful enough, but in retrospect there seems the strong possibility that Abedi planned from the outset to use the bank as a vehicle for political influence. It was of course no accident that First American was based in Washington, the political centre of the United States. The hiring of Lance, Clifford and Altman gave the bank first-rate connections with the Carter regime which Abedi developed with his charitable donations to the Carter Presidential Center and Global 2000. Other notable American political figures appear also to have benefited from BCCI largesse, and that has been reflected in their political statements. Among these are thought to be two noted sympathisers of the Arab cause, the former ambassador to the United Nations, Andrew Young, and Jesse Jackson, the black presidential candidate. Young has admitted that BCCI gave a loan to his consulting firm, which it did not have to pay back. Young explained it as the belated repayment of a retainer he had been promised by BCCI.

Such influence in the highest echelons of American

life may account for the lack of urgency shown by the US authorities in getting to grips with what has been the most serious abuse of their regulatory and criminal procedures this century. As early as March 1981, a former US comptroller of the currency, John Heimann, wrote to the Federal Reserve calling for the closure of BCCI. However, officials of the Federal Reserve have said that they only learned of the secret takeover of First American, the National Bank of Georgia and the Independence Bank of Encino, California, in a telephone call from the US Customs as late as December 1988. A year later, the head of Luxembourg's banking regulatory authority informed them of the loans made by BCCI to CCAH, but the Federal Reserve did nothing. Eventually, in January 1990, the Fed woke up and launched its own inquiry, culminating in the charges of 29 July 1991.

The process of unravelling BCCI in the United States was only really begun when a Washington-based journalist, Larry Gurwin, wrote a marathon article for the Washington publication *Regardie's*. As Gurwin researched his article, the banking regulators became increasingly alarmed, and when it appeared in May 1990, its conclusions must have hit them between the eyes. For years they had accepted claims by BCCI that it had minimal links with the individuals who had begun acquiring shares in Financial General way back in 1977. Now the links were exposed; the share purchasers of Financial General were also owners of shares of BCCI, or had close links with that bank. That was contrary to an undertaking BCCI had given to the Federal Reserve and blatantly against the US law which states that a group of investors may not buy more than 5 per cent of a bank's shares without the Fed's approval.

Investigations by the New York District Attorney's office were put into top gear.

BCCI had taken US regulators and investors for a ride. It had played a shell-game, ducking and diving between offshore locations and companies, using high-flying but meaningless paper. BCCI's tricks in the United States are familiar to fraudsters, but the scale was not. That is why BCCI America was the fraud to beat all frauds.

# 6 Drug Money

The world's multi-billion-dollar drugs money-flow boosted BCCI's turnover for ten years. BCCI, alongside many more respectable banks, targeted Noriega's Panama. BCCI turned money laundering into a high banking art. But Noriega's overthrow would undermine the bank itself.

BCCI opened up in Panama on 22 April 1980 with a royal fanfare at the Hilton in Panama City. The president of the country at the time, Dr Aristides Royo Sanchez, attended to hear a paean of praise for Panama delivered by bank president Agha Hasan Abedi. The bank's vice-president, Alaudin Shaik, was also there and he took the opportunity to have a word with the newly appointed deputy manager of the branch, Daniel Gonzalez. 'The Panama operation should do all it can to increase deposits,' said Shaik. 'This would mean bringing in cash deposits from drugs,' said Gonzalez. 'No problem,' said Shaik, 'just develop the business.'

The Central American state of Panama was well positioned for the rogue bank. It was a short aircraft ride away from Miami and the US mainland, and an even shorter flight over the Caribbean to its financial centre on Grand Cayman. Panama also adjoins Colombia, one of the world's largest cultivators of cocaine.

The country gained notoriety when General Manuel Noriega came to power in 1981. Noriega is believed to have been recruited to the US Central Intelligence Agency as early as 1966, when he was a mere corporal in the Panamanian army. It appears that the United States permitted Noriega's wilder excesses in the belief that he supported US-backed Contras against Sandinista guerrillas in nearby Nicaragua, helped the US cause by backing Oliver North's arms dealing in the Iran–Contra affair, and became a regular player in the worldwide market for illegitimate arms. But drugs money laundering became Noriega's favourite business. At least half a billion dollars of drugs money pass through the Panamanian banking system every year, out of which the country's former leader would have expected a substantial cut.

Among BCCI's early customers in Panama was Noriega's secretary, Marcela Tason, who opened several accounts when the branch opened up. Noriega quickly exerted his influence by having the branch manager removed because he was not sufficiently compliant. That made way for the man who would come to be known as Noriega's banker, Amjad Awan. As soon as Awan arrived, he made it clear to his deputy, Gonzalez, that they should go for deposits from the Colombian drug barons, and he said that Noriega would help with some introductions. Awan had no scruples about the origins of the funds. He told his deputy manager that they would take any amounts of cash or cheques without asking, and that to get the business rolling, they would not charge a commission.

The approach worked. The drugs money poured in and a branch of BCCI was quickly opened in Colon, Panama. Many others followed. Noriega clearly developed a close understanding with Awan – so close in fact that when Awan was transferred to Miami in 1984, Noriega personally protested – in vain – to Abedi, asking for the posting to be cancelled.

Vital to the success of the operation was Noriega's total grip on all authority and power in the country, from the issuing of passports and visas and the running of the Panama Canal to government and, most importantly, the National Bank of Panama. His progress from lowly National Guard in May 1962 to chief of the notorious G-2 intelligence branch and ultimately commander-in-chief of the Panamanian Defence Force was accomplished ruthlessly and efficiently – opponents, it is alleged, were simply disposed of. It was in this atmosphere that BCCI's business was able to flourish without interruption.

Early clients taking advantage of the money laundering facilities were two Americans, Steven Kalish and Bruce Ritch, who had $12 million to be laundered. They were introduced by three close associates of Noriega, who claimed that for a 12 per cent rake-off, they could collect the money from Florida, transport it to Panama and make deposits in the bank of his choice. Kalish and Ritch accepted the deal, and they were taken to see Awan with their cash secured in a bulletproof van following behind. They opened three accounts in the name of Frank Brown, a pseudonym for Kalish. 'Brown' had a passport, driving licence and credit cards to verify his new identity.

That night Noriega entertained his American guests at his mansion in Altos del Golf, and Kalish made him a present of a case containing $300,000 in cash. The following morning, this was deposited in BCCI in an account for Noriega under the name of Zorro. Kalish continued to ingratiate himself with Noriega; he helped the Panamanian leader buy a Boeing 727 for his armed forces, and a helicopter for smuggling out drugs. BCCI strengthened its presence in Panama in 1983, when it bought a Colombian bank with branches in Medellin and Cali, centres of the cocaine trade.

A leading local customer of the bank was drugs

smuggler and launderer Pablo Escobar, who said that he had been introduced to Noriega by Cuba's Fidel Castro and the US fraudster Robert Vesco. Escobar's name would later be prominent in US Customs Operation C-Chase. He is one of the leading players in the Medellin cartel, the largest gang of drugs growers and dealers, which takes its infamous name from the industrial city in Colombia's Andes. Escobar is thought to have started his career in crime as a car thief, from which he progressed to greater things. His associate who was also involved in the operation which culminated in Tampa is Gonzalo Rodriguez Gacha, thought to handle routes to the Los Angeles area. Escobar introduced the Ochoa family to the business of running the distribution network out of Miami. Escobar was elected to the Colombian Congress in 1982 as an alternate member. He has been mainly concerned with lobbies against extradition of suspected criminals to the United States.

Colombia's trade in drugs is vast. By 1984 the annual income for the Medellin groups was estimated to be $1.5 billion. Together with the smaller cartel in Cali, they are reputed to account for the production and shipment of some 60–70 per cent of Colombia's cocaine.

The Panamanian operation flourished for three years. In the course of one month, drug launderers brought $300 million into Panama. Much of this went into local banks, but BCCI took $50 million, and Banque Nationale de Paris (BNP) took $15 million. BCCI's commission on the deal was $1 million, and BNP's $160,000. Noriega's was $15 million.

A particular star of the Panamanian operation was the Colon branch of BCCI whose manager, Wilfredo

Glasse, reported taking $30 million in a single week from a group of drugs money launderers. Five days later a further $9 million came in from First America's Bank, but the bank was so busy counting the $30 million worth of notes that they had to store it in the vault.

Both the bank and its managers did very well out of the success of the Panamanian operation. BCCI only allowed depositors to borrow up to 80 per cent against the sums they introduced into the bank at any one time, so they made a lot out of interest. The bankers themselves also did handsomely out of personal commissions. Awan, for example, who officially earned around $5,000 a month, was able to buy a $700,000 house.

In 1985, the noose was tightening around Noriega's lawless operation in Panama. Noriega sought to appease the Americans by raiding the main Panamanian banks in an operation run by the Americans and dubbed Operation Pisces. Although this netted some $350 million, it is thought to have gone straight into Noriega's coffers. The time was now ripe for the US to mount its own assault on the money launderers. This occurred with Operation C-Chase.

C-Chase, which was performed by US Customs, acquired its name from the Tampa apartment complex which housed the Customs agents. C-Chase was to last between 1986 and 1988, and it was the largest exercise ever undertaken by US Customs. As the incredibly comprehensive indictment shows, every crucial meeting of the operation was recorded on video, phones were wired up and recorded, and cars were continually followed.

US Customs initially used two agents, Robert

Musella and Emilio Gomez, who set themselves up as drugs money launderers for the Colombian cartels who grew and produced the drugs. They would find banks whose services included laundering the cocaine growers' money into the legitimate banking system. Musella and Gomez made first contact with the Colombian Medellin cartel via Gonzalo Mora in Tampa, Florida, in December 1986. Mora explained that using the cover of an exporter of lentils he had been exporting drugs money to the United States for a long time, but the group with which he worked was short of banks to take the money. Musella replied that he could oblige, because he was supported by a large organisation with offices around the United States. To prove the point he took Mora to New York and introduced him to other purported members of the organisation – actually more Customs agents. Mora gave Musella the business and offered him 7 per cent commission. In a short time, Mora introduced Musella to what in the drugs fraternity is called a VIP, that is, a major player.

Roberto Baez Alcaino owned Tiffany's jewellery shop in Los Angeles and was a major dealer in Colombian cocaine. Musella met him in style, flying into Panama's international airport accompanied by the beautiful Scandinavian Kathleen Erickson. She was introduced as his associate and fiancée but was in fact another undercover agent. The next day Mora took Musella and Erickson to a BCCI branch in Panama. He explained, 'It is easy to work with them, they have branches all over the world and have no objection to receiving large amounts of cash.' An account was opened in the name of IDC International and Musella made their purpose clear to the manager, Akbar Bilgrami. 'We are an international operation and our purpose is to launder money produced by drugs trading.'

In the course of 1987 the operation expanded quickly. The cash was first collected from many US cities, then deposited in US banks and finally sent by cable to the IDC International account with BCCI in Panama. At the same time, blank, signed cheques drawn on this account were sent by Musella to Mora in Medellin before being negotiated in a friendly foreign exchange house. While Panama's drugs money trade was being closely investigated, Noriega was living it up, courtesy of Awan, who took him on a jaunt to the gambling dens of Las Vegas in March of that year.

To penetrate deeper into the Medellin organisation, in November 1987 Musella told Mora, with whom he was now in very regular contact, that he wanted to do some bigger deals. Mora could not make the decision himself, but said he would contact his two immediate masters, 'Don Chepe' – a pseudonym for Moncada – and Rudolph Armbrech. Bigger deals meant more sophisticated laundering, and Musella set up a meeting with Amjad Awan, BCCI's laundering expert. The two men met at the Carlos on the Grove Restaurant in Miami and Musella explained to Awan that these new clients would be 'as important to Awan's bank as Lee Iacocca was to Chrysler, the only difference being that Iacocca sold cars and his clients sold cocaine'.

Awan swallowed the bait, but said the laundering technique used by the Medellin barons was risky; he told Musella that he could offer a safer technique. 'We collect cash in the US and transfer it via cable to France or London where it is used to issue fixed term deposits. These certificates are used as collateral to obtain loans, which are then transferred by cable to Panama to be credited to our current account. You can continue to take funds from this current account as you do now.'

In March 1988 Musella met with representatives of the Medellin cartel at the Hotel Cariari at San Jose in Costa Rica. The cartel's top man, Pablo Escobar, was absent, but his representative, Javier Ospina, attended along with Mora. The money launderers occupied four suites at the hotel, one of San Jose's largest, and each of the four had a woman on his arm. Musella and Gomez had two agents for company, while Mora and Ospina had two Colombian escorts.

When they met by the pool at six in the evening, Musella explained the laundering arrangements, and the part BCCI would play. 'BCCI is a very powerful bank,' said Musella. 'Our contact there [Awan] has great experience in dealing with VIPs and he has also had many years as General Noriega's personal banker.' That was enough to swing Ospina into the cause. Ospina said that organisations he worked for had between $12 and $20 million to launder.

The laundering was planned to make use of BCCI branches in London and Paris, and Ospina and Mora were told that Armbrech and Moncada would need to go to the European cities to open accounts. In May 1988 the cartel godfathers had a final meeting with Awan and Bilgrami at the bank's offices in South Florida to check the details of the laundering operation and to receive letters of introduction.

The Colombian party which eventually made it to Paris on 22 May 1988, included frontman Mora and his wife, Rudolph Armbrech who ran Pablo Escobar's finances and could make decisions on his behalf, and Javier Ospina who worked for Moncada and Escobar.

The group was met at BCCI Paris by Nazir Chinoy, the manager of the Paris branch, accompanied by two colleagues, Ian Howard, who despite his name is a Pakistani, and Sibte Hassan. Chinoy explained to the men from the cartel how the system worked.

Couriers carrying suitcases of dirty money would go to BCCI branches around America at a pre-arranged time, and swap them with identical empty suitcases carried by bank officials. The money would then be transferred by cable to BCCI in London with instructions to credit the Paris branch. They in turn would issue fixed-term certificates in the name of Rudolph Armbrech who had opened three accounts at the branch. BCCI in Grand Cayman and Nassau would create a loan guaranteed by these certificates of deposit, and the loan would then be transferred by cable to Panama and credited to Moncada and IDC International. Musella would send signed blank cheques against these accounts to Mora.

On 27 May 1988 the barons went on to London where they were met by Asif Baakza who opened further accounts for them. The cartel grew increasingly to appreciate Musella's skills and laundering system, but the political situation in Panama was worsening as the United States tightened the noose on Noriega. Musella suggested changing the system to cut out Panama, and Mora went to BCCI Tampa. He took Awan's and Bilgrami's advice and decided to make Tampa and Europe the two focuses of the US laundering. A complex money loop was devised to beat regulators who in any event could not possibly check so many transactions.

All funds collected in the United States would be sent to Tampa by cable. They would then be telexed to BCCI Luxembourg, through a New York bank. From

Luxembourg the funds would go to London where fixed-term certificates of deposit would be issued. The CDs would be used to guarantee loans made to different companies which the cartels controlled. The cartels would in turn move their loans to their current account in Tampa, from where they would be sent to BCCI Uruguay. At this point the cartels in South America could get their hands on the money either by going directly to the bank or by taking out a cheque which they could negotiate on the Colombian black market through foreign exchange dealers.

The organisation in London to be used for the laundering operation was called Capcom Financial Services, whose current director was Syed Ziauddin Ali Akbar, the former treasury manager at BCCI in London. In early July a scheme was devised for linking up BCCI offices in London with those in Nassau in the Bahamas which would involve Asif Baakza and Capcom. The funds for the Capcom scheme would come from General Noriega who was facing drugs charges and wanted his money moved out of Panama.

In February 1988 in Florida Noriega had been indicted for drugs and laundering offences. On one occasion he was accused of conspiring to import and distribute more than 1 million tons of marijuana into the United States. The chief witness in the case said he had passed on to Noriega almost $1 million in bribes between 1983 and 1984 in return for a diplomatic passport, a multi-million dollar letter of credit and safe passage for large quantities of hashish.

On the second occasion, Noriega was charged with accepting $4.6 million to allow Colombian ships with over 4,000 pounds of cocaine to pass through Panama to the United States. It is also claimed that he permitted the Colombians to establish a cocaine processing plant in Panama.

In early August, following a discussion between Swaleh Naqvi and Dildar Rizvi, the bank had established an account for Noriega at Capcom, called Finley International, and on 16 August Noriega's money was transferred to Switzerland and Germany. In the course of the next month the money moved around Europe and the United States, through many bank accounts and banks. In the middle of September it arrived in London, and on the same day it moved to Capcom in New York. The $20 million spent the next six months oscillating between London and New York, although most of it went through Capcom, the BCCI affiliate, rather than through BCCI itself.

UK Customs assisted the undercover operation in London. In September 1988 the agent came to London and placed some relatively small amounts – $1 million and less – with BCCI. But the meetings were put on video and the car drives filmed. BCCI set up some new companies, one of which was called Hardiman, for the deal. The money came from the United States via Liechtenstein, to the Leadenhall Street headquarters in London. By now it was common practice for BCCI to create a certificate of deposit to the value of the deposit, and in this case the comparable loan was made from Nassau in the Bahamas. The loan would not be repaid, and the certificate of deposit moved to Nassau and the books were balanced. The money deposited in London was lost through Capcom, whose futures and options business was so large and fast-moving that sums of this magnitude can be lost within seconds, and no one had to explain or account for it.

While this was going on on the UK side of the Pond,

there were some signs of nervousness among BCCI's drugs money launderers in the USA. One over-zealous bank clerk is reported to have told senior BCCI manager Bashir Shaikh that some of the accounts were drugs-related and should be closed. According to an indictment from the Middle District of Florida, Shaikh replied that to do so, BCCI might as well shut down the entire Panama branch. Bilgrami took the same approach when someone else expressed a doubt.

What the clerk did not know was that the drug laundering operation had been discussed by the bank's chief executive, Naqvi, at a special meeting in Bogota, Colombia, four years earlier when, it is claimed, they debated the fact that a significant proportion of BCCI targeted deposits were from drugs money. No one had any intention then of closing down such a lucrative source of business.

The clerk's nervousness was well justified, because US Customs were about to pounce, having now got detailed information on the origins of the drugs, the routes they took into the United States, the men laundering the proceeds and the banks which were prepared to clean them up. The eventual trap proved as clever and as well organised as the rest of the operation. Customs had to bring both the suppliers of the drugs and the launderers of the money together, and their excuse was a wedding party.

The cartel chiefs and the BCCI men were told that Musella and his lady friend Kathleen Erickson were going to get married. The wedding, which was set for 10 a.m. on 9 October 1988, would be held at the Innisbrook Golf Club and Hotel in Tarpon Springs, Florida, and all the men with whom the couple had been dealing so amicably and profitably over the last two years were invited. The watchful Naqvi ensured that the operation would be less than a complete success when he forbade the BCCI general manager to attend, on the grounds that senior people should not be too obviously linked with these kinds of account.

To spare the women's feelings, the agents managing the operation segregated the men from the women. A hen night was held in the hotel dining-room and there was a stag party for the men in the centre of Tampa. Ten limousines driven by undercover agents took the men to the NCNB Bank building in the centre of town that evening. The party was to be held in the penthouse on the top floor, but the lift stopped on the second floor, and all the guests were arrested by federal agents. They were then driven in the same limousines to the county prison.

The news was released to the press by William von Raab, the US Commissioner of Customs, and the Federal Prosecutor, Robert Genzman. They announced that eighty-five suspects had been arrested, of whom some had been charged with conspiring to import illegal drugs into the United States, and others with laundering money produced from the sale of illegal drugs. BCCI was charged with laundering $18.8 million-worth of the proceeds of the illegal traffic of drugs. Forty other banks were put on notice by the US authorities: these included some well-known names such as Manufacturers Hannover Trust Company, Republic National Bank of New York, Security Pacific and Wells Fargo.

The bank itself was charged as well as nine officers of BCCI. They were: Akbar Bilgrami, manager of the Latin American organisation; Amjad Awan, his number two; Aftaab Husain, operations manager for Panama; Nazir Chinoy, Sibte Hassan and Ian Howard from the French operation; Asif Baakza from the corporate unit in London; and other officers from BCCI in Los Angeles.

The bank was split over how to fight the case. Some argued that they should fight it on the grounds of unfair entrapment, an argument which had been used successfully by John DeLorean, the car designer, who had also been subjected to a sting in California. Others contended they would minimise the bad publicity and embarrassment by plea-bargaining. The latter party won and the bank admitted guilt and entered a plea bargain. It was given a $14.8 million fine which one observer described as a mere slap on the wrist and led to Senator John Kerry, the chairman of the Senate subcommittee on terrorism, narcotics and international communications, sending the judge an angry letter. The BCCI executives were sentenced to terms in prison of up to fourteen years. The cartel chiefs appear to have got off lightly. It is now being suggested by Congressional investigators that they had a tip-off before the arrests and withdrew funds from the bank.

Over the two-year-long operation, the Customs agents took the opportunity of arresting some of the Panamanian participants where it would not threaten their ultimate goal, which was to finger the bank. One victim was the Alcaino family. The Alcainos had a sardine export company, which sometimes put cocaine instead of sardines into the tins for delivery to the United States. In March 1988 Alcaino told Musella, who was visiting the family's Pasadena mansion, that he wanted him to launder $500,000 so that he could build a covered tennis court and an underground garage for his two Rolls-Royces and two Mercedes. Musella created a number of companies through BCCI which made 'home improvement loans' to Alcaino. Alcaino also used Musella to launder $50,000 to finance the Super Flyweight World Title fight between Gilberto Roman and Sugar Baby Rojas which took place on 8 April 1988. Again, this involved Musella making loans, this time to Antillas Promotion of Miami.

Musella pumped Alcaino for all he was worth, and drugs dealers revealed that his cocaine came from Gonzalo Rodriguez Gacha, also called El Mexicano. Shortly afterwards, Alcaino and his wife Gloria were picked up collecting a consignment of sardine tins stuffed full of cocaine in September 1988. The incident ruffled some feathers among the cartel chiefs, but they were reassured that their operation with Musella was not threatened.

The hand of General Noriega can also be seen in the activities of Jordanian arms dealer Munther Bilbeisi, who was a major customer of BCCI. Bilbeisi had been smuggling coffee between 1982 and 1986 and he had used BCCI to avoid export taxes, fees and taxes in South America and to avoid US coffee import quotas and sanitation inspections. An internal report from Lloyd's of London, the insurance institution, said that BCCI provided a 'flexible system of payments to foreign associates in Central America'. Because Bilbeisi's import and shipping documents were 'necessarily incomplete or defective' he and his associates needed unquestioning acceptance of such items to insure prompt, safe payment to associates in Central America.

Bilbeisi's BCCI contact was Abdul Sakhia who, according to the Lloyd's report, 'ran a bank within a bank'. Sakhia issued three loans amounting to $2.5 million to Bilbeisi's companies without security. He also borrowed more than $4 million from BCCI which 'was paid directly or indirectly to various persons or companies identified by the US government as being closely connected with or controlled by Manuel Noriega'. BCCI's Miami office also issued twenty-seven letters of credit worth $79 million to Bilbeisi although he only drew on about $8.5 million.

As early as 1983 'any reasonable investigation into Bilbeisi's operations would have uncovered that Bilbeisi's coffee business had used phoney letters of credit issued by BCCI to finance his smuggling', according to a report from a House of Representatives judiciary sub-committee in the United States. In the end the US Justice Department did not issue its indictment for tax evasion against Bilbeisi until August 1991, and that was after the expiry of the five-year statute of limitations on most of the coffee-smuggling operations.

Panama is now bringing two separate actions against Noriega and BCCI whose disregard for the law when conducting business is succinctly summarised in one of the indictments: 'The operations of the BCCI Group in its dealings with Manuel Noriega constitute a racketeering operation of unparalleled scope, international in its reach and totally ruthless in its evasion of banking, fraud, disclosure and common and code laws of numerous nations, including the United States.'

For good measure Noriega, who is now languishing in the Municipal Correctional Center on 137 Avenue in Miami having been unceremoniously toppled in the US invasion of Panama in 1989, also faces charges alleging a catalogue of murder, theft and corruption. In the dry legal jargon of one of the indictments, during his period in office Noriega and others conspired 'unlawfully to convert and cause to be converted to his or their own use money, funds, property and other valuable assets belonging to the plaintiff [Panama].'

Noriega's alleged campaign of murder and torture against priests and opponents continued throughout his leadership and has been much investigated. But his financial operations and his total reliance on the services of BCCI to assist in the systematic plundering of his country's coffers are equally notorious.

On 19 January 1982 Awan, it is alleged, accepted instructions opening an account in Noriega's name but using over $1.3 million of National Guard funds. The instructions specified that the details of the account – No. 03002781 and called M/L No. 2 – should be kept secret at all times and only Noriega was authorised to give handling instructions.

No opportunity, it is claimed, went begging when Noriega wanted to make a few extra million dollars. On one occasion he even instructed the former chief of the Panamanian Air Force, Major Jose Hilario Trujillo, to sell eight military aircraft for $7 million and deposit the money in one of Noriega's rapidly burgeoning bank accounts. On another occasion, the man who had pledged himself to exercise his power as leader of Panama 'honestly' ordered $800,000 to be diverted from a government fund set up to help the struggling Panamanian farmers. It is alleged that Noriega then instructed the general manager of the Banco de Desarrollo Agropecuario to endorse the cheques and bring him the cash. The bank proved to be an exceptionally lucrative source of ready money for Noriega who is said to have removed more than $1 million from its vaults in this way.

BCCI's willingness to accept customers and money

without asking questions had made them the natural bank for Noriega, and they handled the delivery and movement of so much hard currency in as cavalier a way as they conducted all their business, according to written evidence given by the congressional investigator, Jack Blum. Blum quotes an unnamed informant, 'Y', now thought to be Syed Ziauddin Ali Akbar.

'BCCI stayed out of the cash-handling business because it was too expensive. The bank did not use armoured cars to handle the transfer of excess cash.

'Y carried the cash himself in the trunk of his car and did not worry about being robbed. He said that Panama at the time was quite safe.'

With the money safely in his personal account, Noriega then gave instructions for it to be laundered. Half a million dollars were transferred to BCCI's Cromwell Road branch in London (Account No. 03016120). Over the next four years further sums were transferred to Cromwell Road until in February 1986 $3,248,063.33 were moved to another BCCI branch in Edgware Road where Account No. 03001734 had been opened.

Personal expenses such as the payment of Noriega's own Visa cards as well as those of his wife, Felicidad, and daughters Thays, Sandra and Lorena, were paid out of another Edgware Road account (No. 01010571). Between February 1986 and January 1988 the family managed to run up bills of $223,281.73 in shops like Toys'R'Us, Saks Fifth Avenue, and Jordan Marsh – not the sort of shopping the National Guard of Panama would reasonably have been expected to undertake. In November 1987 alone Sandra Noriega – now Mrs Beauchamp – was clearly in no mood to stint herself and managed to charge $24,946.43 on her gold card, including $5,000 at Christian Dior in Paris, during a four-day binge. According to documents deposited at the Miami court the shopping sprees took the family from Panama to Las Vegas, Tokyo, Hawaii and Venezuela during the summer of 1987. The case against BCCI is that the bank was perfectly well aware of the personal nature of this expenditure.

There was plenty left in the account, though, after the shopping, and the false trail had to continue being laid, so both Edgware Road accounts were moved to Luxembourg, first into one account and then into another (Account No. 01164492); the balance in February 1988 was $14,877,667.86. But the funds scarcely had a chance to earn more than a few thousand dollars' interest before they were on the move again, this time to the Union Bank of Switzerland in Zurich and the Deutsche Sudamerikanische Bank in Hamburg, Germany.

Just in case anyone at the National Guard dared to check on the state of the funds, the National Bank of Panama opened an account in the name of Findlays, Findlay International Company or Finley's International Ltd, showing a false deposit of $23 million to cover – so it is alleged – the real whereabouts of the money.

Meanwhile, in September 1988 the money was again travelling the world: from Germany the balance of over $12 million moved to an account at the Middle East Bank in London under the Findlays cover name, to be joined by a little over $11 million from the Swiss bank. All the time BCCI was making funds available to the Noriega family. It is claimed that other funds were channelled through BCCI accounts in the name of Noriega's wife and daughters in Sloane Street, Hyde

Park Corner and at BCCI's headquarters in Leadenhall Street in London.

The case brought by the government of Panama against BCCI is that the bank maintained a branch office in Miami 'for the purpose of expediting these and other transfers of funds' and that for much of the time Awan's position as regional manager and his assistance were 'essential to these transfers'. The indictment reads: 'It was Awan who controlled the relationship of BCCI with Noriega and his clique, and thus these transfers were directed from Miami while Awan was in Miami . . . they were directed by what the BCCI Group termed LACRO, its Latin American and Caribbean Regional Office.'

For the record, it is thought that Noriega's annual salary never exceeded $50,000 during his twenty-eight years with the National Guard and the Panamanian Defence Force, yet it is alleged that he managed to amass a net worth in excess of $300 million. Panama is claiming damages of $6.5 billion plus costs.

# 7 Trading with Terrorists

The busting of the bank has exposed a rotten carcase, swarming with parasitical arms dealers, terror groups and power-hungry security services. The vile stench released infected the bank's financial structure through and through. Its customers included Mossad, the Israeli security service, international terrorist Abu Nidal, the CIA and the Iranian-backed Hezbollah terrorist group, the governments of both Iran and Iraq, and secret services of the United Kingdom, France and Switzerland. With its roots so firmly entrenched in the Middle East, BCCI did good trade out of the arms business between people who in public professed hatred and in private shared bankers and letters of credit.

We now know that Arab terrorists bought weapons from Mossad in deals run by a BCCI bank manager which used BCCI financial support. BCCI staff also assisted Arab terrorists to smuggle arms between the US and the Communist Eastern bloc by providing fraudulent documentation and finance. And, most surprisingly of all, Arab terrorists also bought Israeli-made weapons using BCCI financial support.

The first parasite to nibble at the putrefying carcase was Ben Banerjee, an expatriate Indian and former commercial pilot who had obtained a licence to deal in arms in the United Kingdom. Banerjee lived in the Buckinghamshire village of Olney and owned a company called BR & W Industries. He was a frequent visitor to BCCI in London in the late 1970s, where staff came to know him as 'the old tradesman'. He was a reliable source of letters of credit, and always went through a manager called Shafiqur Rahman Khan at BCCI's Hyde Park branch, one of the key London branches.

'Banerjee would sell anything to anyone, anywhere,' said Ghassan Qassem, the young Syrian-born BCCI bank manager assigned as gofer to handle Banerjee's account. Banerjee got on well with Qassem, in whom he often confided once he had had a few drinks. He once told Qassem that 'the most beautiful thing was being in a Beirut hotel room and looking at the sky and seeing it red from all these bullets. He said he was desperate to continue seeing that sight because it meant more orders for him.' Qassem recalls that Banerjee had sent a single container to Lebanon carrying two separate shipments of arms – one to the PLO and one for their enemies, the Hezbollah. Banerjee was paid for each shipment, and the two groups carried on killing each other.

Banerjee's contacts were far-flung. He was known to the British security services, and acted as an intermediary between arms manufacturers, other dealers and end-users in France, Turkey, the Eastern Bloc, Argentine and Korea, as well as the Middle East. In one deal, Banerjee had arranged the illicit shipment of American TOW anti-tank missiles to Iran, and he was one of the brokers involved in the Irangate scandal.

In 1981 Banerjee introduced his friend Shafiqur Rahman Khan to a prospective new client, Samir Najmeddin, who said he was a representative of the Iraqi government and wanted to set up an account. He was passed on to Qassem whose upbringing in Jordan, where the family had gone shortly after Qassem was born, was thought to put him on the same wave-length as the new client.

Qassem made the necessary arrangements and Najmeddin's account was duly opened. Shortly afterwards, $48 million were transferred from Najmeddin's previous account at Midland Bank's 431 Oxford Street branch, where it had been for the previous three years. Qassem recalls, 'At the time, this sum was the size of a branch, not an account.'

BCCI opened a total of twelve accounts on Najmeddin's behalf. They also went to a firm of accountants on Brompton Road, in Kensington, called Rawi & Company, and organised an offshore trading company for Najmeddin, registered in Panama and headquartered in Warsaw. The company, which was named SAS Trade & Investment, after the initials of the three named directors of the company – Shakir Farhan, Adnan al-Banna, and Samir Najmeddin himself – was supposed to be a company for international trading in facsimiles, computers and office equipment.

Four years later Qassem learned that Shakir Farhan was not the seller of office equipment that he claimed to be but the arch-Palestinian terrorist leader Abu Nidal. Najmeddin had also given him a phoney story. Instead of being a representative of the Iraqi government, he was the treasurer and financial brains behind Abu Nidal's organisation. Adnan al-Banna, a relative of Nidal's, made no pretence – he was just a name which meant nothing to the young banker, for the official company house records.

In fact the al-Banna name might have alerted Qassem, had he been more politically aware. Abu Nidal was born Sabri al-Banna and only adopted the *nom de guerre* of Abu Nidal or 'father of the struggle' in the 1960s, when he joined the PLO. He later became a Maoist-style communist following military training in North Korea and China, and split with the PLO in 1973 when its leader, Yasser Arafat, suggested that a policy of 'progressive moderation' might bring about a peaceful agreement with Israel.

Nidal then set up his own organisation, the Fatah Revolutionary Council, totally dedicated to the destruction of Israel and prepared to use any means to achieve this. He has been called the most dangerous man in the world. His campaigns of terror have killed more than 900 people in at least twenty countries and his name is known and feared across the globe.

Abu Nidal's forte does not seem to have been finance, and he left that to his aide, Najmeddin, while retaining power of attorney over all the BCCI accounts. In 1981 Nidal came to London in order to transfer $500,000 into his newly opened personal account and he was to return only twice more during his involvement with BCCI. On his last visit to the UK in January 1985 he had his briefcase stolen in his hotel lobby in mysterious circumstances. Nidal reported the incident at Paddington Green police station, but they did not question his identity and he left the country immediately afterwards.

Between 1981 and 1986 Najmeddin was to become one of BCCI's Hyde Park branch's most valued customers. He also developed a close friendship with Ghassan Qassem, who was struck by the man's shyness: 'He was very, very humble, very soft-spoken, he is afraid of his own shadow. When we walk, he's very timid and not a man of power or personality. But he treated me as a father does a son.'

Once his account was opened, Najmeddin opened a letter of credit for $30 million to Ben Banerjee, who supplied him with ammunition from Turkey and rockets from France. The deal went smoothly and BCCI made a huge commission from the profit. For the next five years Najmeddin used BCCI for all his letters of credit. Each one over the value of half a million dollars was approved by the Central Credit Committee, a group of four senior UK management figures led by Swaleh Naqvi.

Najmeddin's main European base was in Switzerland and later in Poland, but when he was in London he was given *carte blanche* by BCCI to use their offices for his own business. This involved sending coded messages and receiving replies on a daily basis. Qassem recalls that occasionally staff were employed for whole days, simply dealing with Najmeddin's telexes. Qassem was too preoccupied with financial considerations to consider the purpose of these telexes: 'No one mentioned that this was a terrorist account. This was the biggest account we had. We had to make sure that they were never upset or we would lose them. If we lost them we were finished.'

Najmeddin began as a purchaser for Nidal, but he gradually became a trader and broker in his own right, supplanting Banerjee, and selling arms to other governments and terror gangs. He is known to have supplied night vision devices to Argentina during the Falklands war, artillery shells to the Iraqi army and handguns, shotguns and ammunition to the Iraqi police.

Despite his dedication to the violent overthrow of the Israeli state, Najmeddin developed working relationships with several Jewish arms dealers. In 1982 he entered a deal to ship military equipment to Abu Nidal's base in Poland, where the Fatah Revolutionary Council could operate freely provided they did not carry out attacks on Polish soil. Najmeddin's associates were Leonard Berg, the president of a police equipment concern called HLB Security Electronics Limited, and Solomon Schwartz, the director of a company called Global Research & Development; both men were Jewish Americans based in New York who had links with Mossad.

The export of arms from the UK to Poland was illegal, but Najmeddin went with Qassem to a British accountant based in Geneva called David Mitchell (who was subsequently charged with offences relating to Barlow Clowes) and asked him to arrange a number of letters of credit to the total value of $10 million for SAS Trade & Investment, saying that he wanted to export pipeline spares to the Eastern Bloc. Qassem told the accountant that an offshore company was needed because this kind of shipment to Poland was forbidden by the British authorities.

On the surface this seemed in order, and the accountant planned to use an offshore company whose name suggested it dealt in pipeline spares. But he got cold feet when it transpired from documentation that the eventual destination of the shipment was the Polish Ministry of Defence. The accountant says he reported the incident to the British Consulate in Geneva, who told him, 'You're mixing with some very dangerous people.' This indicates that British Intelligence already knew something about Najmeddin's work.

The deal proceeded through BCCI without the Geneva connection and a letter of credit was arranged, stating falsely that the shipment's destination was Mexico. The arms were bought from Britain, Belgium and the United States, along with other devices for shipment such as electric prods, used for crowd control and torture. The consignment was loaded on to a privately chartered jet at Kennedy airport, but on 21 February 1984, as the plane was about to take off, US Customs officials swooped, arresting Schwartz and Berg.

As far as US Customs were concerned, this was a

conventional bust. Schwartz was a known racketeer with Mafia connections, who had been under surveillance for some time before his arrest. But when he was arrested Schwartz claimed that he was acting on behalf of the Pentagon, who asked him to obtain two Soviet P72 tanks from the Polish army, offering to pay $4–6 million for each tank. Schwartz said that the arms were to be sent as an exchange deal with the Poles. The CIA denied any involvement, but questions were still asked by the *New York Times* – why should the Poles risk an international incident to import arms they could have got legitimately from the Russians?

The key to the episode is Najmeddin's involvement. The Poles certainly did not need the weaponry being smuggled – it was, after all, fairly routine equipment and they had their own manufacturers and sources – but Abu Nidal most certainly did. Nidal also had the money to pay for it.

According to one source, the deal was set up between the CIA and Najmeddin to finance the defection of a Polish general. The general had demanded $1 million to come over to the West, and if the deal had worked out, the CIA would have provided Najmeddin with arms, which would then have been shipped on to Abu Nidal in Poland. In exchange, Najmeddin would have paid the $1 million to the Polish general, who would then have defected.

In 1989 Schwartz and Berg were sentenced to ten years apiece for racketeering, wire fraud, conspiracy to violate the Arms Export Control Act, exporting arms in violation of that act and related offences. They were ordered to pay fines of $700,000 each. Early in 1991 the Court of Appeals for the Second Circuit reversed three of the counts – for racketeering, wire fraud and defrauding the Munitions Control Office – but affirmed the rest of the convictions. The assessed fines were reduced by $277,000 to reflect the reversal of three of the counts and the sentences were remanded for consideration in light of the disposition on appeal.

The Irangate deal was proceeding at roughly the same time, also through BCCI and also involving the CIA, and in fact Schwartz broke his bail bond in order to sell arms to the Iranians. In the course of the court case, he had claimed to know Oliver North.

The bank participated in a number of other incidents of arms-trading in the Middle East where unusual bedfellows came together. For example, in 1985 Najmeddin set out to acquire some Israeli-made Uzi machine-guns, telling one of his contacts, a man who owned a weapons shop in Mayfair, that he wanted 200 of these. The shop owner said he knew someone who could oblige and the following day an Israeli came to the bank branch office. According to Qassem, 'He talked about how he was going to get the guns from Israel. He made a big scene, and said, "I can only get you twenty now, and twenty every month." Najmeddin said, "No, I want them all in one go, otherwise I'll go somewhere else."' The Israeli agreed to the terms, and agreed payment, which amounted to $48,000 for the guns and $80,000 for the silencers. 'They came to my office in BCCI and received the cheques from me and gave me the bill of payment. They knew who they were selling to.'

The deal was concluded successfully, and the Uzis were shipped out of Heathrow on a Swissair plane. However, Qassem was later told by British Intelligence that the company the Israeli owned was a front for Mossad. The incident poses a number of questions. It seems extremely unlikely that the Israelis did not know who was behind Najmeddin, so were they freelance traders who did not care who bought as long as the money was good? If they were Mossad-linked, could the weapons have been bugged or spiked in some way?

The bugging evidence may be strengthened by another trade that went through the bank. In April 1986 Nezar Hindawi made his infamous attempt to blow up an El Al flight from Heathrow to Tel Aviv by planting a bomb in his pregnant girlfriend's luggage. It appears that Najmeddin was responsible for buying the electronic exploding devices from Israeli sources, and Qassem reckons that Hindawi was foiled because the devices had already been bugged.

Although Iraq was providing the Fatah Revolutionary Council with a base, Najmeddin was not averse to selling arms to both the Iraqis and their enemies the Iranians. In 1984 Najmeddin had meetings in London with members of Iran's Logistics Support Centre, which was based at 4 Victoria Street, next door to the Department of Trade and Industry. As a result, contracts were signed committing him to supply arms to the value of $25 million.

Negotiations for the deal were carried out using BCCI telex machines. In fact this was contrary to BCCI policy which strictly allied itself with the hardline Arab Iraqis, but it seems that the policy was never really policed. In 1984 the Iranian-backed Hezbollah group was found to have an account in BCCI's High Street Kensington branch, where they were being looked after by an Iranian officer. The account was closed and the officer was sacked. However, nobody tried to stop Najmeddin selling equipment to Iran.

Qassem thinks that the arms sent to Iran may have been spiked by Nidal before they were sent. 'Sometimes they would sell out-of-date products by changing the expiry date on the boxes. Sometimes they would pretend to be selling large amounts of equipment and would negotiate for a long time, so that Iran did not receive anything while Iraq did. But sometimes the organisation needed money, so they had to sell arms.'

It is perfectly possible, however, that Najmeddin was applying the philosophy of the market-place and not asking any questions. Iran was regarded as a pariah in the West and the United States, and she was desperate to find arms for her war with Iraq. BCCI was never one to turn away a profit, whatever the source of funds.

Syria was also a problem client for Najmeddin, but in 1985 she was anxious to obtain an Arwen 37 riot-control weapons system. Najmeddin contacted Royal Ordnance, the sole manufacturer of this item, and stated that he wanted to purchase the weapons system on behalf of the Syrian government. The application was turned down, apparently at ministerial level, for political reasons. Undeterred, Najmeddin scoured the embassies of London and within a week, an official at the Sierra Leone embassy had been paid £20,000 to authorise an end-user certificate stating that the weapon system's destination was not Syria but Sierra Leone. The documentation was presented to Royal Ordnance and this time the export was approved. Soon afterwards, Royal Ordnance realised that they had been duped, and called in Scotland Yard to investigate. By this time, however, the shipment had already left the country, bound for Rotterdam and from there to the Middle East.

Najmeddin worked with Qassem for four years, apparently keeping the young bank manager in the dark about his real business the entire time. But in 1985

Najmeddin seemed to have an attack of bad conscience, according to Qassem. 'He tried to hint to me indirectly that he had put me in a wrong position, trying to apologise. He used to say things to me sometimes, indirect things that made no sense. For example we used to talk about Palestinians sometimes, while having dinner. He used to quote things and examples just to be heard saying it . . . he couldn't say anything to me openly because he did not know what the reaction would be, what danger he would put himself into – whether it would cease the operation with the bank.'

That was just before Najmeddin's cover was blown in the French magazine *L'Express*, which quoted information on him from a leaked FBI report and openly accused him of being Abu Nidal's financier. Najmeddin made every effort to excuse himself to Qassem, claiming that the article was all lies. He went to court in order to clear his name, and as the magazine could not summon the FBI to substantiate the leaked report, he won.

Still, Najmeddin no longer felt safe dealing through BCCI in London, and in early 1986 he began to withdraw large amounts of money from his BCCI accounts. The smallest of these withdrawals was $5 million dollars, and the money was transferred to accounts held in Switzerland and Poland. Within two months Najmeddin had left the bank completely. He continued to trade from Poland for another two years until the US government pressured the Poles into expelling him. On 14 January 1988 Samir Najmeddin left Poland and his days as an international arms trader came to an end. Today, he is believed to be living in Libya, along with Abu Nidal. Both men are wanted by Interpol.

More than a year after Najmeddin and Nidal pulled

out of BCCI, in mid-1987, Qassem was summoned to a meeting at Flemings Hotel, Mayfair, where he met an MI5 agent who asked him to cooperate with the secret service's inquiries into his bank. He agreed. He says the process of vetting was 'very sophisticated' and he claims the security services 'had tried many others even Mr Naqvi' in their bid to find someone they could rely on. Qassem refutes later suggestions that MI5 used information in their possession to pressurise him to assist, and says he did it out of duty to the UK. Qassem quickly discovered MI5 had been interested in the affairs of BCCI since 1983 and already knew a lot.

Qassem cooperated with the security services for three years, and he says the identity of his client came as a complete shock to him; although he admits he was puzzled when he learned that the 'Iraqi' had married a Palestinian, he had no reason to suspect Najmeddin. 'The security services said you have been dealing with people in whom we have great interest and these guys are very, very dangerous.' As a condition of co-operation, Qassem says he obtained a letter from MI5 and MI6 saying 'they appreciated my assistance in helping the government in controlling the activities of terrorist groups and drug traffickers who were destroying human lives. I think it involved the Prime Minister and the Home Secretary because MI5 and MI6 never issue letters.'

MI5 were not alone in using Qassem. Between 1987 and 1990 he provided documentation for several intelligence agencies including those of France, Switzerland and the US. 'They came to me with a list of things and said they wanted precise details of everything. I was giving them banking information that was on file: details of individual transactions, everything you could imagine that took place that was illegal. I never photocopied anything. I used to give them originals.'

The authorities' interest went wider than Nidal and terrorism. They also wanted to know about BCCI's drug traffickers. 'In my branch [Sloane Street] there were about ten accounts that were involved in drugs. Some of these accounts were handled by head office. These accounts belonged to the relatives of people in head office and so the finance was approved.' He tells of one drugs dealer, related to somebody in the bank's international division, who had an account in Qassem's branch. This account was credited with $500,000 a week from one of three BCCI branches, Luxembourg, Panama or Miami.

Once, when the drugs dealer failed to pay an outstanding debt, Qassem tried to make inquiries about the account. Someone in BCCI's head office warned the drugs trafficker that he was being investigated, and the same night he flew by Concorde from New York to London. He arrived at BCCI Sloane Street at 9 a.m. the next day and closed the account.

Other accounts at Sloane Street were highly suspicious. Qassem handled ten numbered accounts belonging to ministers and government officials from Latin America. Money poured into these accounts but cheques were never issued from them.

The depositing of large amounts of cash into BCCI branches had been a regular procedure until 1988, but then the United Kingdom passed legislation requiring banks to take details from anyone depositing or withdrawing more than £10,000 at one time. This did not seem to bother some BCCI branch managers, and in 1989 a drugs dealer came to the bank's Hyde Park branch and paid in £1.5 million in cash over the counter.

Qassem says that the manager took the risk because there was something in it for him, as there had been in the past.

In 1989, following a two-year investigation, the security services decided that they had the evidence they required and they went to the Bank of England and auditors Price Waterhouse, who mounted the Project Q financial examination of the bank. The team included a partner in Price Waterhouse, two senior BCCI officials and Roger Pierce, a Scotland Yard Special Branch officer. Their reports alleged financial irregularities and the unauthorised transfer of millions of pounds for arms deals. Details were sent to the Bank of England accordingly.

In August 1990 the Q team sent a letter to John Bartlett, head of the Bank of England's supervisory section dealing with banks in North America and Europe. In January 1991 they sent Bartlett a copy of their interim report, identifying a core group of eleven customers and forty-two accounts, many linked with Abu Nidal. In the following month the Q team referred two suspect accounts to Special Branch under the Prevention of Terrorism Act. The Q team is understood to have continued in operation until the Bank of England closed BCCI, when its findings were handed over to Touche Ross, the liquidators.

Qassem finally resigned from BCCI in March 1990. Living a life of deception was giving him nightmares and he felt he could no longer carry on. He had expected no payment for his services but was shocked that it had become known that Operation Q was named after him. Qassem now lives in hiding, bitter at the betrayals of the last decade – first by Najmeddin, then by MI5, which left him exposed to the possibility of retaliation from former colleagues at the bank.

BCCI had connections with the security services and arms dealers the world over. For example, it assisted the CIA in the financing of arms to Iran and paid Nicaraguan Contra rebels with the proceeds, in what later became known as the Irangate affair. Adnan Khashoggi, the Saudi arms dealer, indicated in a 1987 interview with the US Congressional panel investigating the affair that $17 million worth of finance for the deal passed through accounts which he held in BCCI's Monte Carlo branch, and that some of the profit was to go to the bank itself. Bert Lance has given testimony to a US Senate Committee that he was visited by CIA agents seeking details of the bank's Irangate involvement.

As part of the same arrangement, in 1984, Colonel Oliver North opened three accounts at BCCI's Paris branch in the name of a Panamanian-registered shell company, Devon Island. The accounts were meant to link in with a transaction worth $10 million involving the sale of American TOW anti-tank missiles. The profits from this deal were then transferred to a Saudi Arabian branch of BCCI and paid to Adolfo Calero, the head of the Contras.

BCCI's willingness to turn a blind eye in order to make a profit perfectly complemented the operations of an intelligence agency which would break the law to further what it saw as the national interest. BCCI was the ideal bank to finance covert operations – it had branches not only in major cities but also in the most remote areas of the world.

The CIA transferred funds to Mujaheddin rebels in

Afghanistan during the Soviet occupation, using BCCI in Pakistan. As it turned out, the money was embezzled at every stage of its passage and used by some of the rebels to finance their own drug-smuggling operations (the profits being laundered back through BCCI, of course). Nevertheless, the passage of funds to Afghanistan was always bound to be a fraught operation, and it is difficult to see how the CIA could have targeted its money any more precisely.

The CIA also used BCCI for routine business: through branches in London's Cromwell Road and Edgware Road – the same branches used by Noriega to launder drug money – it paid 500 British CIA contacts, including senior figures in politics, industry, academia, banking and the media. These contacts or 'monitors' provided the Agency with information – for instance, details of British arms sales and overseas contracts, sometimes before the deals were even made.

In the mid-1980s Robert Gates, deputy director of the CIA from 1986, described BCCI, with some glee, as 'the bank of crooks and criminals international'. Nevertheless, while other regulatory bodies in the United States were keen to close the bank down, the CIA did much to prolong its existence. In September 1986 the CIA prepared a memorandum detailing BCCI's criminal activities and its secret ownership of First American Bank. The memo was circulated to federal law enforcement agencies and to the Treasury, but no mention was made of the CIA's own involvement with BCCI, and no prosecutions ever resulted from the memo. The CIA has since reported that it did not report this to the Federal Reserve.

In 1988 US Commissioner of Customs William von Raab sought information on the bank from Robert

Gates. Raab recalls that he was given no access to the memo and received no documents other than what he calls 'well-written pablum', information that was already widely available. Several weeks later Raab found out from Customs agents in Britain about the CIA's use of BCCI, and has since accused Gates of being 'less than candid' about the affair. He complained that Federal Reserve and Customs investigations into BCCI were consistently stonewalled by other US government agencies. He accused the US Treasury – then headed by James Baker – of being 'lackadaisical and worked over' by 'some of Washington's most blue chip influence pedlars' and said that the Department of Justice had been 'pounded' by lobbyists for BCCI.

Many government security services had intimate links with BCCI, but none was closer than Pakistan's. In the 1970s BCCI was heavily involved in the financing of Pakistan's attempts to build its own nuclear arsenal. This came about through Abedi's close ties with General Zia, then President of Pakistan. Over the next fifteen years, a series of attempts was made to obtain nuclear components, with varying degrees of success. BCCI transferred cash and gold in order to finance the operation, and arranged air freight, shipping and insurance.

In 1983 the head of Pakistan's nuclear programme, Dr Abdul Qadir Khan, was arrested in Holland on charges of trying to steal blueprints for a uranium enrichment factory. BCCI provided for his defence, paying all the expenses of his legal counsel.

BCCI is also thought to have underwritten the illegal export of nearly $1 million-worth of computer equipment for Pakistan's nuclear programme between 1982 and 1983. Moreover, in 1987 a Pakistani-born Canadian was indicted in the United States for conspiring to export speciality metals to Pakistan for use in a nuclear bomb. Documents found in his house showed that the deal involved the use of London and Toronto branches of BCCI (Luxembourg).

BCCI was supposed to have had its own secret service, the so-called 'black network', a global intelligence operation and enforcement squad, ruthlessly dedicated to the furthering of BCCI's cause throughout the world. The black network was allegedly a 1,500-strong squad based in Karachi, consisting of hand-picked individuals who underwent a one-year training course in psychological warfare, spying techniques and the use of firearms. They would then be dispatched all over the world, implementing BCCI's illegal activities, whether they were drug trafficking, gold smuggling or international terrorism.

Whether or not anything as systematic as the black network actually existed, BCCI seems to have been no stranger to the techniques of espionage and surveillance. For example, US law enforcement agencies investigating the bank repeatedly claimed that the bank employed people to stake out the investigating officers and to tap their phones. BCCI's protocol officers were responsible for making sure that whatever the bank wanted, it got – by means of either bribes or terror. In the United States, bribery was used to secure business deals or to gain access to industrial and military secrets. In Pakistan, the preferred method was terror. As one former BCCI employee told *Time* magazine: 'The Pakistanis were easy to terrorise; perhaps we might send someone his brother's hand with the rings still on it.'

BCCI was prepared to unleash its own terror on unreliable protocol officers. In 1990, when an officer was found to be selling his house and liquidating his assets, his brother was killed and brigands came to his house and raped his wife. The officer fled to the United States, where he remains in hiding. US investigators have little hope that the man will testify against BCCI – if he is ever located.

Since the bank's closure, two journalists investigating BCCI have died in mysterious circumstances. Joseph Casolaro was researching aspects of the 'October Surprise', and Anson Ng was uncovering BCCI's activities in Guatemala. What these journalists may well have discovered is that BCCI's tentacles stretch further and are more dangerous than anyone had imagined.

# 8 Guilty Secrets

During the mid-1980s the secrets of BCCI's meteoric growth started to surface. The accountants were looking a bit more deeply than usual into the company's affairs because its treasury had crashed into loss. The regulators had finally stumbled on this anomalous institution and were scratching their heads over it. The State security services were also nosing around and discovered that the bank had some interesting customers. Finally, law enforcement authorities had picked off some key managers in a money laundering operation and were now watching its every move. Word in every financial centre was that this was an untouchable bank, and the pressure began to tell at 101 Leadenhall Street, BCCI's City headquarters, where staff felt they were in a state of siege.

The regulatory noose around BCCI would begin to tighten in 1984, when the Luxembourg authorities first raised doubts. They carried the greatest burden since the bank's holding company was incorporated in Luxembourg. The Luxembourg Monetary Institute (LMI) could not believe the speed of BCCI's growth and was convinced it did not have the management to control it. BCCI's assets had increased almost eightfold in seven years, from $2.2 billion in 1977 to $16 billion in 1984, and even the best-run organisation experiencing that sort of growth would creak at the seams.

The 1984 Vienna conference was regarded by senior bank executives as the high point of BCCI's fortunes. On that occasion Percival Twitchin, a BCCI director, gloated over the capital fund which had grown by 26.5

per cent on the previous year and now stood at $810 million. He observed to the assembled mass of managers that for the first time the shareholders had not contributed. 'It's from our own efforts,' said Twitchin, adding that the bank was 'pretty proud' of another statistic: the net income, expenditure and profit figures in relationship to assets. 'The profit pre-tax and pre-loan loss provisions showed a return of 3.29 per cent on total average assets for the year, and it was 3.35 per cent the year before, and by any stretch of the imagination they are fantastic banking statistics,' he chortled. 'I would not be surprised that we are maybe at the peak there as we grow in size. I can't believe that we will ever get back to 3.5 per cent, but 3.3 per cent isn't bad either.'

In fact 1984 was to mark the start of the decline of BCCI's fortunes and the increasingly close attentions of banking regulators around the world. Luxembourg had seen enough to know that BCCI's managers were not equipped to manage the rate of growth, and they also knew that Abedi had a compulsive need to expand the bank. But in 1984, BCCI was already having some difficulties in the highly speculative area of options trading which lost them $105 million.

Pierre Jaans of the LMI reacted to the worrying rate of growth, and tried to galvanise other regulators, notably the Bank of England, but to no avail. He tried again the following year when he sought to persuade the Bank of England to assume greater responsibility for BCCI. In 1985 the LMI decided to commission Price Waterhouse to carry out a detailed investigation. This found significant losses which had gone unrecorded, although at the time this was only put down to incompetence by BCCI's managers.

In their bid to find some way to share the onus of

BCCI's regulation, the Luxembourg regulators suggested that the bank spread around the responsibility of regulation and adopt a new three-legged structure. This would mean that the bank would be incorporated in its three main places of business, the United States, the United Kingdom and the Cayman Islands. But it never got beyond the planning stage. Regulators continued to let BCCI slip between the regulatory cracks, and the bank pursued a policy of exploiting this in the United States when it craftily bought Financial General.

The Bank of England, which should have stepped in at this point, given that BCCI's operational headquarters were in the City of London, decided that the commitment in time and money was too great and passed the buck. Elsewhere in the world, fraud was requiring regulators to yield to pressure. US law enforcement agencies were forcing the Swiss to open up Ferdinand and Imelda Marcos's bank accounts in Switzerland containing several hundred million dollars, and this would become an important precedent for future efforts to attack banks handling illicit flight capital.

There were already plenty of signs that all might not be well with BCCI's operations. For example, police officers in Britain investigating the Johnson Matthey banking failure found that a number of their suspects had accounts at BCCI. The police had gone to BCCI for information about a large deposit made by a well-known individual. A policeman involved in the investigation said, 'We had information saying he had deposited a large sum of money but I had enormous difficulty getting any information out of BCCI. They said, "We don't know anything about this chap, he hasn't got an account here and we don't keep any records."' The incident was extremely significant in the context of the individual who had obtained money by fraud from the Johnson Matthey Bank and put it into BCCI, the policeman said. The police did not follow up BCCI's involvement in the Johnson Matthey banking crash, although one source suggested that in the course of the investigation, arrests of senior BCCI directors had been considered.

By 1984 Bank of England officials were already putting the word about that BCCI was not a bank one could do business with. On one occasion, the chairman of a bank with links with the Middle East who was seeking a banking licence was given a confidential piece of advice to steer clear of BCCI by a senior Bank of England supervisor.

A scandal in India in 1986 provided some more early smoke, although quick action by BCCI succeeded in stifling the fire. It may have been an anomaly that BCCI should have been represented in India, given the two countries' political hostility and Abedi's closeness to Pakistan's leading politicians, but Abedi had ingratiated himself with Indira Gandhi, using his family connections with the Maharajah of Mahmoodhabad and possibly even bribes. The bank was allowed to set up a branch in Bombay in 1985, shortly after Mrs Gandhi's assassination but, within a year, the bank had clashed with the authorities. The allegations against them had a familiar ring – money laundering and links with espionage circles.

According to the former director-general of India's Revenue Intelligence, B. V. Kumar, BCCI had sought to get round the country's foreign exchange regulations which prohibited anyone from remitting foreign exchange out of India without prior permission of the Reserve Bank of India. Kumar said BCCI staff were doing 'some underhand dealings' and breaking its Conservation of Foreign Exchange and Prevention of Smuggling Activities Act. His officers raided the BCCI premises and the general manager and three of his staff were arrested and put in jail. The investigators claimed that BCCI was selling unsigned and unrecorded traveller's cheques to people leaving the country to enable them to dodge foreign exchange controls.

BCCI in London reacted with urgency, even panic, and sent over Nadir Rahim, its manager in London who had the brief for India. He hired Bombay's top lawyer who had the BCCI men quickly released. Said B. V. Kumar, 'Unfortunately they [BCCI] sent in a petition to the Bombay High Court and got a stay order so the cases were only registered, not prosecuted.'

Rahim told the Indian authorities that the arrests had taken place at a time when the bank was extremely busy. The bank had moved into the travel agents where pilgrims going to Mecca for the Haj were buying their tickets, to provide them with traveller's cheques. These had to be signed, and stamped in the passport. 'They arranged to entrap us,' said Rahim. 'They swooped down on one of these situations and they confiscated a lot of traveller's cheques which were not signed that had been there for issue to people still waiting in the queue.' The bank would later be accused of exporting traveller's cheques from Brazil to Paraguay. Those charges were also dropped.

That was only the first of BCCI's problems in India. Indian Customs subsequently investigated charges that the bank had assisted in other breaches of Indian foreign exchange controls. Indians were obliged to return unused foreign currency to the Bank of India when they returned to the country, but it appeared that BCCI was buying back the surplus at a hefty premium.

BCCI also got involved in the underground network run largely by expatriate Indians living in Hong Kong, who used the bank to slide illegally obtained money past the exchange controls by buying and selling Indian companies. According to B. V. Kumar, 'We had the corporate raider, non-resident Indians who were trying to take over big corporations in India. They had their deposits in Hong Kong and against that deposit the advances were being given in India. So actually it was their own money that they were borrowing and the bank had no risk at all. In other words, tainted money deposited in Hong Kong was used through Bombay.'

From the bank's inception, there was some natural mutual suspicion between BCCI and the Indian authorities. But in time, the authorities acquired evidence to support this, and the bank came to be regarded as a real security risk. 'At that time we also knew that this bank was an undercover espionage network for the Pakistan government,' said Kumar, who claims that BCCI's staff were followed 'to establish what their real business was about and the Indian Government was informed. It was only a watch-and-learn operation by the authorities. We alerted and cautioned the government agencies. Once you know that a person is doing this kind of work, you caution others and say beware of this kind of bank. The alert was given. These people were helping to spy on India.' Kumar says he had been in touch with other international security services, which may have included the CIA, and Kumar confirms he met US Customs commissioner William von Raab who shared with him his deep suspicions about the bank.

In the following year, 1987, British Intelligence would learn considerably more about the bank's activities through its London mole, bank manager Ghassan Qassem. This would initiate an international surveillance operation involving several secret services which coincided with a financial crisis at BCCI. The treasury in the bank's head office had run amok and become one of the biggest drains on the bank's dwindling capital. Treasury head Syed Ziauddin Ali Akbar had sold the idea of commodities and futures trading to Abedi as a quick fix for the $200 million loan they had out to the Gokal Gulf Shipping firm, which did not look like being repaid. This went disastrously wrong, losses piled up, and Akbar had to leave the bank.

The full details of the treasury's fraudulent operation were finally documented in the damning Price Waterhouse report which landed on Robin Leigh-Pemberton's desk at the Bank of England in June 1991. It appeared that a treasury within a treasury had been set up which traded disastrously, using customers' names, money and companies for its own account. Price Waterhouse said these shadow names, the so-called 'Number Two accounts', thus escaped the normal audit and 'exposed Sandstorm [the Price Waterhouse code for BCCI] to significant risks and lost considerable sums of money'. Losses made by the treasury were covered up using funds from the Number Two accounts. Just before the auditors came in to check the books, Akbar and his team would let individuals buy options from BCCI and the money would then appear as profit rather than as part of a transaction which might not eventually produce a profit.

Between 1977 and 1985 the total amount of losses and fictitious profits were estimated at $633 million. Price Waterhouse said, 'This is before adjustment for losses of $225 million booked in the 1985 accounts as a result of our treasury review.' Price Waterhouse estimated that $1.3 billion passed through the treasury, which had misappropriated depositors' money without their knowledge, misappropriated funds deposited by shareholders of BCCI Holdings, and created entirely fictitious loans 'of no commercial substance'.

Wherever a new hole appeared, Akbar would use someone else's money to plug the gap. The largest single unrecorded deposit, amounting to $246 million, was made by a bank identified with the name 'Tumbleweed' in the report but now known to be the Faisal Islamic Bank of Egypt.

When Akbar resigned in the same year he took with him crucial documents with which it is alleged that he managed to blackmail his former employers for $32 million, and in October the treasury operations were transferred to Abu Dhabi. This move, which was administered by Price Waterhouse, looked in retrospect like a disastrous error of judgement.

But Akbar was prepared. He set up his own futures and trading operation and invited Abedi to use that for his futures and options trading. Capcom Financial Services, based in London's Gray's Inn Road, was little more than son of BCCI treasury. It had the backing of Christopher Williams, the managing director of Rudolph Wolff Financial Futures, which Akbar had used while he was working at BCCI, and he also managed to bring in some of BCCI's more substantial shareholders.

These included Kamal Adham and Abdel Raouf

Khalil, both with Saudi Intelligence, and Williams. Some of the names of the directors were also familiar. For example, Ghaith Pharaon had installed his brother Hatton on the board. Akbar had wanted to win business in the United States and so he brought on board Bob Magness, one of the elder statesmen of US cable television and founder/chairman of Tele-Communications Inc, and Larry Romrell, a TCI vice-president. The two men were offered a generous package: for Magness that began with a 10,000 share investment and a seat on the board, while Romrell got 110,000 shares and became chairman of the board. Their holdings increased dramatically. In October 1988 both men resigned – a week after Capcom was implicated in the Tampa sting.

Another founding shareholder of Capcom was Robert Edward Powell. He has gone on the record as saying he was set up in business by Kamal Adham in Long Beach, California, running a company called Global Chemical. Adham is also thought to be in business with Raymond Close, former CIA station chief in Saudi Arabia.

Capcom subsidiary Brenchase Ltd, which according to company searches gives its business as a hire-car and taxi operation, was a front for BCCI which paid it $68 million in June 1985 'for an unknown purpose' – chauffeuring BCCI clients, perhaps?

On 17 August 1988 Capcom was expelled from the Association of Futures Brokers and Dealers (AFBD) because they could not satisfactorily identify all the beneficial owners of the shares. In their report to the board, the directors wrote delphically: 'It will be noted that the AFBD did not conclude that Capcom Financial Services Limited was in fact not fit and proper. The directors believe they merely concluded that there might be other beneficial owners about whom they knew nothing. The directors of Capcom Financial Services Limited know of no undisclosed beneficial shareholders.'

One possible source of information which will not be available to any investigating team is the contents of one hundred boxes of files and papers held at a London storage depot. The depot received a request from Capcom Financial Services director Sushma Puri to dispose of the boxes a week before the bank was shut down.

Akbar was to be convicted for his part in the Tampa drugs money laundering affair, receiving an eighteen-month prison sentence in the United Kingdom. He was eventually released in April 1991 after serving six months. At Akbar's trial the judge offered this comment about Capcom: 'I am also satisfied that so far as your company was concerned, there were no previous arrangements. In other words, your company was a clean one.' In 1991 the State of Florida would take a different view when Capcom was indicted in the Noriega drugs trial.

Akbar remains a substantial shareholder and throughout his trial and imprisonment had his legal expenses paid and earned a £10,000-a-month hardship allowance which by January 1991 totalled £270,000. The company also covered itself for hefty fees and set aside $1,550,000 to cover 'legal costs and fees to regulatory authorities' during 1989/90.

Akbar was later to make vigorous protestations of his innocence. Assisted by his solicitor and Capcom Financial Services director Michael Barratt, the two men lobbied the British media, offering strategic interviews to august publications like the *Financial Times* at some crucial moments. This convicted drugs money launderer told the *FT* in August 1991 that he was being made a scapegoat and that he was only obeying orders. Akbar described how a committee chaired either by Naqvi or Abedi met every morning. Naqvi was said to have monitored all the trading, including the bank's Cayman Islands operations through which the treasury trades were booked. 'I was simply a coordinator among several departments. I never originated any deals,' the *FT* quoted him as saying.

But Akbar did not wait to explain further and in September 1991 he made a run for it, only to be picked up in Calais in a joint Anglo-French police operation. Gone was the image of the international businessman with smart suit and tie. In its place was the hunted fugitive in denim jacket being escorted away by French Customs officers. In his hotel room police found documents including bank statements, letters and other accounting notes.

Once BCCI discovered the scale of the treasury losses, the LMI and its boss Pierre Jaans stirred again and asked Abedi what he was going to do about it. To plug the growing holes, Abedi started switching funds around his far-flung empire. In one known deal, the ICIC Foundation, whose purposes were stated as charitable, was leant upon to provide a $150-million 'subvention' for the ailing BCCI bank. That was not going to be enough to keep the bank afloat, and the BCCI president also looked over the water, to the Gulf, for assistance. By now, however, the panic was beginning to set in. It was going to prove a short-lived salvation.

Abedi approached the great Saudi family of the bin-Mahfouz, who controlled the National Commercial Bank of Saudi Arabia, and they agreed to help. But they extracted a heavy price from BCCI, and Abedi's negotiators had precious little room to manoeuvre. It is claimed that Abedi had prematurely told the Luxembourg authorities that he had the new finance and they should not worry further about the bank's solvency ratios. That information got out, perhaps through Abedi's own pride at his achievement, and the bin-Mahfouz lawyers had BCCI in the palm of their hand. Said a close associate of Abedi: 'I differed with him over the need to find new funds since we could have stopped expanding and begun consolidating. But he had made the promise [to Luxembourg]. We were negotiating with Mahfouz's lawyers when the capital terms were being discussed. Because Abedi had committed himself they knew the commitments, so they dictated the terms.'

After a hard fight, Abedi gave the bin-Mahfouz an indemnity against loss, if they wanted to sell their shares. The bin-Mahfouz first bought 10 per cent of the BCCI shares, but they increased their holding to 20 per cent and Abedi started to worry that the rescue would turn into a predatory raid. It is thought that they wanted 30 per cent of the shares which would have given them control. 'They asked for guarantees that whenever they wanted to sell, the shares would be bought back,' said Abedi's associate, who revealed that the deal was underwritten by ICIC. 'It was too big a commitment for ICIC. Abedi's commitment laid the bank wide open . . . it was a very rash promise.'

That Mahfouz deal sealed the future of the bank as an independent entity, because from the moment the bin-Mahfouz took over, they sought to oust Abedi. They had him over a barrel because they knew that even if he didn't like them he would have to make sure they did not lose on their investment. Abedi was in desperate straits. His dream for the bank depended on his keeping control, but the money was draining away and he could see the Mahfouz plan to gain creeping control over BCCI. As an associate of Abedi put it, 'At one stage Mahfouz wanted to buy the whole thing, and that scared Abedi who didn't want to part with BCCI.'

Shortly after the Mahfouz arrangement was agreed, Abedi's health began to falter. Fighting off the powerful and predatory Saudi family had taken its toll. Although Abedi lived in the higher spheres of Sufism, he saw the bank on the ground was failing financially. There were many other pressures, accumulated over the years, now besieging his bank. For example, there was the growing pincer effect of the regulators who had at last got their act together. In December the 'college' of regulators formed a group comprising supervisors from the United Kingdom, Luxembourg, the Cayman Islands, Hong Kong, France, The Netherlands and the United Arab Emirates. Then it was agreed that the bank's two-tier auditing arrangement, whereby the Luxembourg holding company, BCCI Holdings SA was audited by one firm, and its offshore companies in the Cayman Islands by another, was also under attack, and a single auditor took over. This was ever-faithful Price Waterhouse, who had audited the bank's Cayman operation since its establishment. The lead auditor who managed BCCI SA in Luxembourg, Ernst and Whinney as they were then known, resigned, claiming to have been dissatisfied with the BCCI management. It was far too little, much too late.

Agha Hasan Abedi suffered his first heart attack in February 1988. As usual his work-load had been heavy, but he insisted on flying to New York for a staff meeting. Nadir Rahim, the bank's head of human resources, tried to intervene. 'When he was leaving the office I was aware that he wasn't well and I got up from my desk and I said, "You are not looking well, why don't you cancel your visit to New York?"' But Abedi brushed him aside, saying people were expecting him and there was no question of cancellation. He flew to New York in the BCCI corporate jet and returned overnight to put in a full day's work in the office working on decisions about staff postings.

At five o'clock that evening, looking close to exhaustion, Abedi prepared to fly off to Lahore where he had arranged a dinner with President Zia in honour of Sheikh Zayed who was making another visit to the country. Abedi always insisted on personally meeting his most important customer when he arrived in Pakistan. But his eyes were bloodshot, he was running a fever, and everyone in the office seemed to be aware of the risks. Again Rahim, feeling responsible for his president's health, spoke up: 'I felt he was taking chances with his health and I wasn't wrong. He again said, "Mr Rahim, you know that there is no way I cannot go, it is the President of Pakistan, it's a command performance. I can't not be there."'

Abedi arrived in Lahore and as he was dressing for dinner he had his first heart attack. Old friends President Zia and Sheikh Zayed rushed to his hospital bedside, and they were aghast at the tubes and dials keeping their banker alive. For the Sheikh it must have been an even greater shock as he looked down on the man who had guided him through the financial jungles of the world and advised him on his investments. This was no ordinary banker–customer relationship.

The Sheikh ordered that his own plane, equipped

with the latest life-support technology, should remain in Lahore – it was a life-saving decision. Dr Khalid Hamid, Abedi's personal physician, now head of the Cromwell Hospital in London, flew out to Pakistan the next day and former President Carter despatched by private jet the man who had invented heart transplant technology. Dr Hamid coordinated the meeting and it was decided that Abedi would be dead within hours unless he was moved direct to London. He was carried aboard the Sheikh's jet with the BCCI corporate plane flying in formation behind. They arrived in the middle of the night and Abedi underwent immediate surgery.

Subsequent operations, including a heart transplant, an operation to repair a detached retina and surgery to improve breathing difficulties, all left Abedi an enfeebled man. On top of everything his vocal chords had been damaged and his speech seriously impaired. The inspiration and driving force behind BCCI was now confined to a wheelchair, scarcely able to communicate and thus shielded from the storms of controversy which were about to break around him.

# 9 Last Gasp

At the end of the 1980s the bank's future was hanging in the balance. Regulators, accountants and shareholders were wriggling in discomfort at the build-up in evidence of fraud, but pathetic efforts at salvage continued. Whether through buck-passing, or else because security services had now taken charge, everyone copped out.

Price Waterhouse saw at first hand evidence of the financial collapse. They had signed off the 1988 accounts with qualifications about possible future financial penalties over the Florida indictments. The bank managed a net loss of $49 million for the year, but the mystery surrounding the loans was increasing. The following year, 1989, the loss leapt to a massive $498 million. The bank's total assets had risen from $20.6 billion to $23.5 billion, but loan loss provisions had jumped to $600 million from $145 million.

Throughout 1989 Price Waterhouse were sweet-talked by the bank's senior management who gave them soothing reassurances about their determination to bring the bad loans under control, although in March the outstanding loans had risen by a further $150 million.

The bank was flayed with a welter of bad publicity – the money laundering and drugs had replaced good works in its newspaper coverage. The American NBC television news programme revealed documents in June showing how Noriega used the bank to syphon off millions of dollars out of the Panama economy. On 2 October 1989 the bin-Mahfouz family saw that all hope had gone and exercised their option to sell back their holding. Abedi arranged for them to place their stake into the friendly hands of the Sheikhdom of Abu Dhabi, which bought it for $528 million. In fact Zayed himself took only a small part of it. His son Khalifa bought most, some 35 per cent of BCCI's equity, and the Abu Dhabi government's finance department took 29 per cent. The Abu Dhabi Investment Authority chipped in, taking 9 per cent. The Sheikh himself had 3.5 per cent at this time, and BCCI's own ICIC Foundation had 7 per cent.

At the end of the year one of BCCI's best customers, General Manuel Noriega, was overthrown by a US invasion. The White House decided that this Central Intelligence Agency contact had served his political purpose and that his involvement in the drugs world could no longer be tolerated.

The British tax man was also moving in with a warning that BCCI had failed to file correct tax returns. On 14 March 1990 the accountants Price Waterhouse told the bank's directors of their worries. They wrote to say that nothing was what it seemed, loans which had been written into the books as assets had never existed or were now being denied by the alleged borrowers. The names that had adorned the bank's note-paper and loan-books realised they had been abused for the bank's ends and were fighting back. The Rulers of the Gulf states of Ajman and Fujairah, for example, rejected out of hand responsibility for $270 million-worth of loans. A special internal task force was established to 'find out' what could be done.

Price Waterhouse were seen to stir. The firm's partner Christopher Cowan, told Naqvi, BCCI's president following Abedi's illness, in no uncertain terms, to 'meet the customers concerned to understand the nature of their disagreements . . . and provide us with your file on these customers'.

There was even a hostile exchange of letters between the accountants and their much-valued client, BCCI, throughout the spring of 1990. The accountants had woken up to the $750 million exposure to the Gokal brothers' Gulf Shipping group, a string of disputed loans worth $870 million to Credit and Commerce American Holdings (CCAH) and equally doubtful loans worth $477 million to other BCCI shareholders.

The Gokal problem was at the heart of the affair. For years, BCCI's accountants had gone along with Naqvi's solutions, but even they were getting concerned and now they wanted some explanations out of Naqvi. Meetings turned acrimonious when the size of the loans dawned on the directors. Even more terrifying, there wasn't much they could do about it. If they called the loans in, they would have forced the collapse of the Gokal empire and with it the failure of BCCI.

The directors were 'fooled by Naqvi who time and again came to the meetings with some new proposal to give the Gokals more credit', said one insider. These proposals purported to show that the main debt was coming down, but 'all the proposals were phoney'. This inside source says that Price Waterhouse went along with Naqvi's evasiveness and 'never adequately investigated what was really being suggested'. Price Waterhouse is also said to have failed to check that credit lines were cleared and vital documents signed. 'Price Waterhouse often told the directors that the loan was a big one, but never that it was a bad one.' The same applied to countless other loans which went unchecked but, because they were all kept just below $10 million, were not considered important enough to be discussed at board level.

It was already widely observed that the Gokals were spending BCCI money like water, failing to account for it, and losing all management grip on the company. What had been a drive for profitable growth in the early days turned into a push for business at any price. Abbas Gokal had also lost touch with his staff, either through delusions of grandeur or because he could no longer cope. It was now rare for managers who had formerly been treated as equals by Abbas, to get to speak to him at all.

One manager who snatched a conversation with Gokal at this time, mentioned that senior staff, including members of Gokal's own family, were 'stealing blind'. Gokal is reported to have said, 'I don't mind people stealing from me because if they are holding down a position which enables them to steal for themselves, then they're going to try very hard to hold that position. I will only allow them to stay in that position if they're making money for me. Therefore, by stealing for themselves, they're also stealing for me.' This paradoxical position only made any sense if Gokal could control everything that was being stolen, and it quickly became obvious that he could not.

As far back as 1983, managers down the line discovered that when the company went to BCCI to increase its loan, it only received some 90 per cent of the money. It was assumed that the missing part went to the bank's branch managers, and the people working for Gokal. Former BCCI bank officers on the Gokal payroll are thought to have engineered the loan and then taken their cut. In 1984 there was a rumour that the Gokals paid BCCI $25 million in return for a bank loan of $200 million.

Other abuse came to light when one of Gokals' honest managers was put in charge of refurbishing some of the Gokals' time-share chalets at Broome Park in the United Kingdom. He put the business out to tender and accepted the lowest bid, only to be abused by a furious contractor whose bid was twice the one he had accepted. It turned out that the previous manager had done a deal with this contractor, whereby for every £60,000 the contractor charged, as much as £42,000 went to his personal account. Corruption was also rife in the Gokals' Hong Kong office.

There were also some bad investments. For example, Abbas Gokal spent $40 million buying an interest in a Brazilian shipyard. Without examining the books, he thought it was government owned and this would give him control. Later he found that he had bought a minority interest in a family-run business. A subsequent attempt to salvage the situation by a flotation in the United States appears to have been scuppered when a partner tricked him, using critical sensitive information passed out of the company by an employee. This meant he had to find $40 million of ready funds, a fatal requirement for the Gokals, who spent all their cash as soon as it came in. It was at this point that Abbas Gokal began to panic.

In April 1990 Price Waterhouse warned the management that 'certain accounting transactions had been either false or deceitful'. The Bank of England received their copy of the report the day after the BCCI directors but wanted yet more evidence before it dared move. Robin Leigh-Pemberton told the Commons select committee, 'Our view was that even if these transactions added up to individual acts of fraud, it did not add up to systematic fraud.' He continued, 'If we closed down a bank every time we had a fraud, we would have rather fewer banks than we have.'

It is known that information about drugs money laundering and links with terrorists had already been passed to the Bank of England a year earlier, according to Ghassan Qassem. That was when Operation Q was started. It had been preceded by two years of investigation by the security services of many countries, including MI5, who had provided information to the Bank of England about what they had found.

'MI5 realised they had reached a stage when they had completed their investigation. Because they had finished they sent messages to the Governor that the BCCI had to be closed and "Can you do your side?"' said Qassem. The Bank's own team then moved in to investigate ten different sample cases.

Nevertheless, the Bank of England along with the Luxembourg authorities, Price Waterhouse and BCCI itself continued to regard the bank's problems as salvageable, and they recommended a new injection of cash. Naqvi went cap in hand to the main shareholders in Abu Dhabi. But Sheikh Zayed refused to see him, he wanted to see his friend Mr Abedi. So Naqvi turned round the BCCI corporate jet and flew off again to Karachi to collect a wheelchair-bound and scarcely coherent Abedi to do the asking on behalf of the bank. Abedi was so ill that he had to be coached to mouth the right words before he went in to see the Sheikh. It was a request Sheikh Zayed could not refuse.

Price Waterhouse wanted assurances that there was money to underwrite the dud Gokal loans and other treasury losses of the mid-1980s to complete the 1989 audit. They got it from the Sheikh's own adviser, and an investor in BCCI, Ghanim al-Mazrui. He gave them comfort saying that the Abu Dhabi government was 'prepared to provide the necessary financial support in the event that losses arise from realisation of these loans'. The accountants needed to hear no more and the 1989 accounts were signed off again. As far as the outside world of depositors and investors was concerned, all was well with the bank.

Except that there was some small print involved. Price Waterhouse added a rider: 'They [the Government of Abu Dhabi] have advised the directors of their intention to maintain the group's capital base whilst the reorganisation and restructuring necessary for its continuing development is undertaken.' Later, that was to be the accountants' get-out when charged that they had missed the gigantic holes forming throughout the bank's assets. This form of 'weasel words', whose meaning is far from clear in any case, does not look like a full-blooded qualification of the accounts to warn investors of the state of the company. Price Waterhouse later said that if they had done that, it would have started a run on the bank.

By early May 1990, when BCCI announced a loss of $498 million for 1989, it had become clear that the 'restructuring' was failing and the bank was continuing to haemorrhage its capital. The shareholdings were given another shake-up and the Abu Dhabi government put in another $400 million in new equity capital for a controlling 77 per cent stake. With the Sheikh now in complete control, Abu Dhabi wanted to get the regulatory position sorted out once and for all. They decided to introduce a tripartite structure with a PLC in London. This time it was proposed that there should be a PLC in London which would be subject to the Bank of England and wholly regulated in the UK; a company in Hong Kong would deal with business in the Far East; a third sector in Abu Dhabi would handle the rest of the world, including the offshore Caymans operation. Each would deal with the others at arm's length and, according to leading solicitors now representing the depositors, if the scheme had been given time, it might have worked.

The Sheikh summoned the existing management of the bank in London to see him in Abu Dhabi to tell them of his plans. Naqvi knew that he had to get his team over to the Gulf as quickly as possible, and he hired a jet. On board alongside Naqvi were former stars of the bank, like Masihur Rahman, Saleem Sidiqi and Ameer Siddiki. It was a gloomy trip. One of the passengers recalls how Naqvi gave the executives a pep talk saying that they really must apologise and convince the Sheikh that nothing like this would ever happen again. If they failed, he warned them gravely, they could be 'dropped down a well.'

To implement the plan a committee was set up which would organise the transfer of the bank's main centre of operations from London to Abu Dhabi, effectively sidelining the bank's corrupt but brilliant financial wizard, Swaleh Naqvi. The committee that took control in Abu Dhabi got some new chief executives on board, had some note-paper printed for the newly styled companies and even began to arrange for customers to alter their account details to fit in with new companies that were to be created. It appeared to be a touch of professional management which had been quite contrary to the bank's history of phoney paternalism.

The Sheikh's decision to move the bank over to Abu

Dhabi was greeted with particular dismay in the Rahman household. Masihur Rahman, the finance director of the bank, was married to an American who had no interest in submitting herself to the Arab world's restrictions on a woman's freedom. His wife put her foot down and refused to move. Rahman resigned but he made as much of a stink as possible, perhaps in the hope of getting a payoff – a favourite BCCI way of keeping disgruntled employees quiet. For example, he demanded his share of the Staff Benefit Fund – the internal pension fund, set up by Abedi in the early days of the bank to top up employees' benefits when they left or retired. By this stage, the fund had been plundered dry to make good the gaps left by earlier adventures in the treasury department. Rahman himself had organised the emptying of the Staff Benefit Fund and it surprised many that he should have made this request. His attempts to extract money out of the empty fund through a legal action were clearly doomed and his subsequent protestations to the media are regarded rather cynically by insiders. The move to Abu Dhabi started a massive shake-up at BCCI and a major redundancy was started.

The committee tried to pay for the Gokal loans with staff overheads. In the early summer, when operations moved over to Abu Dhabi, BCCI made 800 of its 1,460 UK staff redundant. This was part of a larger 4,000 worldwide redundancy. Platitudes were no comfort to people who had worked far harder than the call of duty required to help the family bank for so long. Those who remained were told that the UK business would remain a vital part of the BCCI structure, and 'it can be made more profitable through a slimming down'. The bank's staff pointed a more accusing finger. On 19 June Vivian

Ambrose, a member of BCCI's UK regional inspection department, wrote to Labour MP Tony Benn with the bitterness of a man who has seen his dreams smashed. He told Benn: 'The apparent incompetence of the bank's executives and higher management is surpassed only by the widespread corruption and nepotism within the organisation.' The letter was to have an unexpected passage through the British parliamentary system. Benn passed it to the high-profile Treasury on the grounds that it was about banking. But they claimed it was more about conditions of work than finance and passed it to the Department of Employment. There it appears to have got lost in a bureaucratic muddle. When the fate of the letter came out in the House of Commons it was evident that ministers had passed the buck on this particular bank, hoping perhaps to put off the time yet again when somebody would have to act on this rogue in the midst of the British system.

Later, Sheikh Zayed put in a further $600 million to cover bad debts and that was followed in October by a further call for $1.5 billion to cover other loans. BCCI had become a black hole. The Gokals – in at the start – were now, towards the end, identified as the principal bad debtors. Price Waterhouse eventually produced a bad debts figure of $1.2 billion for the Geneva-based shippers.

The decline of BCCI was watched over with growing anxiety by the Gokal brothers in Geneva. They met regularly with the BCCI directors to discuss their loans and seemed to be safe from drowning. But when it was announced that the Sheikh of Abu Dhabi had taken control of their bank, a frisson of fear shot through the staff. It seems that relations between the Gokals and the Sheikh had never been particularly good. No one knew exactly why but there was a suspicion that Abedi had told the Sheikh about the bribing incident a decade before which had opened up BCCI's exposure so dramatically. In any event, the Gokals' Gulf employees knew that they were terribly exposed and in for trouble. 'You could feel the fear go through the company. It was a tangible thing,' an employee noted.

Lurid stories multiplied. Word went round the company that representatives of the Sheikh and the Gokals had been close to blows when they had met in Geneva to sort out the loan. According to one observer, 'Some hard words passed between them, there was virtually a fist-fight.'

Fear turned to panic and irrationality in the Gulf Shipping boardroom and Gulf staff sought a mystical salvation to their financial problems. 'As things got worse, going to the mosque got more and more important,' observed one manager. 'I used to say, "What's going to happen here?" and they would say, "If God is good, such and such will happen."' The religious enthusiasm also infected their business, and some managers prayed before they did a deal. This practice, called *kaddesh*, involved the manager opening the Koran at random three times, and the passage that he turned up would determine whether and how the deal was done. On one occasion the company actually paid more than was necessary to charter a ship because the reading of the Koran dictated it. (Senior managers of the family were unperturbed and in fact promoted the manager.) Observance of the feast of Ramadan became stricter, and Gokal family members were expected to fast. According to one non-Muslim manager, 'For the first week of the month at least, damn-all business got done because everybody was asleep, especially in the summer because the fast was very long.'

The widespread view at Gulf was that the Sheikh of Abu Dhabi had resolved to call in the loan which the company owed to BCCI on the first day of 1991. The Gokals would have realised the damaging effect of this on their company, although it is possible that the Sheikh may not have known the total amount of Gulf's indebtedness to BCCI. When he did, it was too late, and the size of the loan pulled down not just Gulf, but BCCI as well.

What the Sheikh saw may have been seriously distorted by Naqvi. Naqvi is known to have inflated the Gokal loan with penal interest which he kept recorded in his private files, thus inflating the BCCI assets. In fact, this was just another paper exercise, because the Gokals had not been able to pay any of it back for a number of years. At this time Price Waterhouse found that Naqvi and Abbas Gokal had together arranged to spread the $1 billion-plus loans around 750 companies 'so that the auditors thought the account had come down, whereas it had not. It was window dressing and he shouldn't have done it in the view of one insider.'

This was only one of a number of desperate measures to which Gulf Shipping and BCCI had resorted in order to decorate their respective sets of accounts. Managers report that the group went to BCCI to remortgage everything they could lay their hands on. The Gokals also tried to sell off parts of the business, including its Broome Park time-share estate. It even considered an offer from George Walker of Brent Walker. Shortly before the holding company, Gulf International Holdings SA, filed for administration in Luxembourg, the company began 'making up charter parties' according to one Gulf manager who left at this time.

The charter party is an agreement between two parties whose documentation can be brought to the bank as guarantee for an upfront loan. Banks only agree to do charter party arrangements with shippers whom they can trust to repay them, and on deals which look solid enough to ensure the money will come through. 'A lot of those were presented to BCCI and certainly it must have been obvious after the first one had failed that there was a fraud. But even after that, more were presented and more were accepted.'

There is some evidence that trading between the Gokals and other companies and executives in the BCCI empire may have been irregular, and contributed to the bank's downfall. In 1985, for example, the Gokals had to repay a loan to BCCI and so sold their 50 per cent share in Sharjah Luboil to Ghaith Pharaon, a major recipient of BCCI money. The company's stake in TradiGrain was also sold to Pharaon for the same purpose.

The plummeting credibility of the Gokals in the late 1980s meant that they could no longer cover their exposure by making further deals. As it became harder for them to find people who would do business with them, they cut their prices to a point where the deals were no longer profitable. In the words of one broker: 'In the last nine months, we did at least twenty deals of Gulf/Japan [these are safe and uncomplicated contracts] where they lost a minimum of $3 a ton. Each deal definitely lost $3 million.'

The degree to which the shippers sank the bank remains a matter for conjecture. What is certain is that from an early stage the Gokals were not repaying their loans. The bank appeared not to insist on their repayment, and was prepared to doctor its books to show they were still performing. Ultimately, those loans had reached an untenable proportion of its balance-sheet and the cover-up was out of hand. According to the Price Waterhouse report circulated on 22 June 1991, over the fifteen years the Gokals banked with BCCI, they had 750 accounts, whose turnover was $15 billion.

For at least ten years, Naqvi had played the game of hide-the-Gokal-loan with remarkable success. No one knew better how to use corporate structures, paper companies, legal niceties and the like to slip bad business through the cracks. He did it with nothing more than a sharpened pencil and voluminous paper files.

On 28 July 1990 Naqvi packed the whole lot into a few suitcases and took them over to Abu Dhabi. It was his last fling. When Price Waterhouse prepared their next report – on 3 October – the accountants had moved to Abu Dhabi and found Naqvi and his files. Now they could outline thirty pages of 'inappropriate transactions' by senior members of the BCCI staff.

The Price Waterhouse report gave Sheikh Zayed a picture of the antics that had gone on at his bank, and the day after it was produced, he decided to act. On 4 October Abedi and Naqvi resigned at a full BCCI board meeting and the Sheikh launched his own inquiry under the vengeful eye of accountants Ernst and Young who (as Ernst and Whinney) had been elbowed out of the bank by Price Waterhouse years earlier.

On Christmas Eve 1990 Sheikh Zayed warned darkly that his government would terminate any agreements to save the bank 'if any criminal or illegal activity was involved'. It was not clear then whether he was referring to the bank or to its shipping clients.

Round the world, there was no doubt that BCCI had had a fair share of its own illegality.

- Florida was the jurisdiction of yet another BCCI case where a businessman Munther Bilbeisi had been indicted on charges of tax evasion and coffee smuggling. BCCI was his bank.
- In Argentina the Central Bank had already ordered BCCI to start winding up its activities.
- In March the Federal Reserve Board had ordered BCCI to sell its stake in CCAH through which it controlled First American.
- In Italy, BCCI found itself linked to the Banca Nationale de Lavoro whose Atlanta office was implicated in providing fraudulent loans to Iraq.

Considerations about the closure of the bank were put on hold in the latter part of 1990. No one in the Treasury or the Bank of England wanted to risk relations with an ally in the Gulf while British and American forces depended on it for cash and political support in their clash with Saddam Hussein. Matters in Threadneedle Street went back on hold until 4 March 1991 when it was time for another report. The Bank of England went to the bank's own firm of auditors, Price Waterhouse, for a secret, independent, examination of the BCCI books under section 41 of the Banking Act. Price Waterhouse appear to have had no problem with the conflict of interest, thinking perhaps that official action was now so imminent that anything they could do to salvage their reputation would be to the long-term good, and the tougher their report the better.

The report certainly put off the evil day, and gave Sheikh Zayed yet another opportunity to spend some of his many millions. In May the Abu Dhabi government agreed to hand over promissory notes to the value of $3.06 billion to cover problem loans.

Six weeks later, on 22 June, the section 41 Price Waterhouse report landed on the Bank of England's desk. It told of unimaginable frauds in every section of the bank, ranging from treasury to Islamic banking. Well-manicured hands were wrung in horror. The following week there were confabs in Threadneedle Street. The Governor of the Bank met the Chancellor of the Exchequer, Norman Lamont, and even the Prime Minister, John Major, and told them of his decision to shut down the bank. On 28 June phones buzzed between the Bank of England and the Federal Reserve. The Governor prepared the Fed to move against the bank in a joint operation the following week. The Federal Reserve Bank sent people to the United Kingdom to coordinate the final moments. Hong Kong was unhappy, however, arguing that their BCCI organisation was clean, and there was no reason for such draconian action. Rocking the boat at this time was frowned on, however, so the Colony kept its peace and obeyed orders. It is interesting that no one got on the phone to the Ruler of Abu Dhabi, the bank's biggest shareholder. The Bank of England took this stance for reasons which as yet are unclear. It has been suggested there was a lack of communication between the UK regulator and Abu Dhabi.

Five minutes' walk away from the scene of these top-level decisions, at 101 Leadenhall Street, Leonard Kingshott, former chief executive of Lloyds Bank International, was preparing for the greatest challenge of his banking career. On 1 July he had moved in to BCCI to shake up and reorganise BCCI plc on a salary of

£150,000-plus a year. Four and a half days later he would be out on the City streets without a job.

On 2 July senior supervisors at the Bank of England were in session all day to work out the logistics of closure. Across the Atlantic the Federal Reserve Bank was likewise briefing its agencies. The following day, BCCI's biggest debt burden hit the rocks. The Gokal family's Gulf International Holdings had notched up loans of the order of $1.2 billion in the course of its eighteen years with the bank, and now it had also been rumbled. On 3 July it was put into administration by the Luxembourg authorities.

Friday, 5 July, the day the Bank of England moved, saw the Bank of England in court. Orders to appoint liquidators and administrators had to be obtained in the High Court in London and there was a nail-biting time while similar orders were obtained in the Cayman Islands and Luxembourg.

Liquidators Touche Ross had been on standby since 8 a.m. The message was: be ready to handle 'a major business failure' and drop whatever you are doing. It could not have come on a worse day for the massive firm – a big presentation was to have been made at a partners' meeting.

The final message to swoop came as most bankers in the City of London were enjoying their lunch. As soon as the Luxembourg court approved the order, an announcement was flashed on to the Reuters screens around the world: BCCI to be wound up. Official.

Touche Ross teams descended on branches throughout the United Kingdom, shutting them down, while other teams carried out the same action around the world. There would be no sleep for the top partners for the next three days.

As soon as the announcement was made, the twenty-five UK branches of BCCI were visited by either a partner or senior manager from Touche Ross. The local managers were told to ask their staff to collect any private property, to remove no papers and leave the building in an orderly fashion.

Most of the staff were returning from the special room set aside for prayers when the news reached 101 Leadenhall Street. At first they were bemused, but then people panicked. Some started 'rushing about' trying to get some cash from the tills. They knew it would be their last chance.

That afternoon, the two senior Touche Ross partners, Brian Smouha and Christopher Morris, met with the Bank of England supervisors at Threadneedle Street to organise liaising with the Luxembourg authorities and the Cayman Islands regulators. A centre of operations was established at Leadenhall Street and throughout the weekend the key teams were put together. The insolvency team was led by Morris, while Smouha took command of the bank auditing side. Management consultancy people secured the rather old-fashioned BCCI computers and tackled the credit card business. Leading City solicitors Freshfields were appointed to handle the legal side.

Another team was established at the Cannon Street office to deal with the bewildered staff who continued for days to stand on the doorsteps trying to find out what was going on. The weekend gave Touche Ross a vital breathing space. It became a round-the-clock operation involving about 300 staff. By Monday an advice line had been set up for customers and the following day Touche Ross were able to offer a free advice line to businesses.

It was the largest bank closure in history and it stretched Touche Ross to the limit. The firm even had to draw on manpower from some of the other major High Street banks to set up another team to handle letters of credit.

Not all countries shut their branches immediately. In Pakistan they stood by their man and, apart from the presence of armed guards on the doors, it was business as usual – although in the coming weeks Abedi would be refused permission to start a new bank.

The Hong Kong authorities decided to keep BCCI open in the Colony and even put out a statement urging the 40,000 depositors not to withdraw their money, claiming the bank was essentially perfectly sound and viable. Two days later they were forced to change their minds, close the bank down and appoint liquidators. Depositors were outraged. Many had taken the authorities at their word and left their money in the bank only to see it all disappear. There were violent demonstrations on the streets and some even started hunger strikes.

The BCCI closure set off a panic-run on the jittery Hong Kong banking system. The Hong Kong financial establishment had enough to worry about regarding 1997 and subsequent Chinese control without a bank crash, and rumours abounded about which would be the next bank down. Citibank was caught in the panic. Standard Chartered, a British bank, was going to lose its licence, said the Colony's jeremiahs. The bank reassured its customers that this wasn't true by keeping its doors open three hours later than usual and issuing vouchers to those still waiting in line. But it still suffered a £230 million run on its deposits.

There was a suggestion of panic within the United

Kingdom too. A run on the tiny Southdown Building Society in East Sussex was fuelled by the 'everything is going to collapse fever' and investors started queueing to withdraw their savings. Later it was said that the BCCI collapse was nothing more than a pretext for a disgruntled employee who had lost his job and wanted to cause trouble. In the hot British summer of 1991, it took very little to ignite dangerous panics. Some minor secondary mortgage lenders also feared a run and the Bank of England stepped in with a lifeboat scheme.

But what of the man whose genius had infused BCCI? On 15 July the bank's founder, Agha Hasan Abedi, broke his silence in Karachi. With a composure that colleagues had come to know and worship, he said, 'I don't hold myself responsible because I have not had anything to do with the affairs of BCCI for the past three years.' Unfortunately that still left the previous sixteen years unaccounted for.

# 10 Shut-down

Abedi's complacency was out of fashion. The timing of the closure took everybody unawares. Most people assumed that another infusion of cash from the Sheikh of Abu Dhabi and at least one more accountants' report would keep the BCCI hulk afloat for a while. In their rush to the courts, even the Bank of England's lawyers were caught off guard. Freshfields' reputation for immaculate presentation was marred by the crossings-out and hand-written passages on the documents requesting closure, and some of its affidavits had yet to be sworn. For an institution with a reputation for stateliness rather than speed, this precipitate action indicated that something serious was afoot.

So it was. It is generally believed that the Bank of England was moved to act by the spectre of an indictment from the Grand Jury in the County of New York within a matter of weeks. It would be a very bad show to be caught napping by the Americans, who had never had as many BCCI branches as the United Kingdom, and were now gung-ho with threats and insinuations that they had evidence that would by itself sink BCCI. Indeed, in the months before the closure, the Bank had had officers from the New York District Attorney's office banging on its door demanding evidence, and had sent them away like naughty boys for wanting to look at teacher's cribs. Were they now to let the aggressive Manhattan upstarts win the day? Some at Threadneedle Street would also rationalise the urgent closure by saying that criminal prosecutions resulting from the Grand Jury indictment would spark an uncontrollable run on the bank.

The *Banker* magazine was in no doubt when it wrote on 14 September 1991:

'What appeared to galvanise the Bank of England into action was the acute embarrassment it would have felt if the New York District Attorney had acted first against BCCI. Morgenthau had his evidence and was determined to use it. But if the indictments he brought against BCCI on 29 July had been made before the Bank of England had moved, there would have been a run on BCCI and UK regulators as chief supervisors would have looked incompetent. Timing was critical.'

Robin Leigh-Pemberton told the Select Committee that what had made him change his mind was the greater detail of the fraud revealed by Price Waterhouse in its June 1991 report. With all the aplomb of a distinguished City man, Leigh-Pemberton pronounced that 'the culture of the bank was criminal'. That upset the feelings of the new owners in Abu Dhabi, as well as the thousands of quite innocent employees round the world, and the Governor, only just converted to the view that the City could have a seriously fraudulent bank in its midst, was later to soften his line.

The spectre of the Manhattan Grand Jury turned out to be quite as threatening as the Governor of the Bank of England must have feared. Brimming with pride that his men at 1 Hogan Place, Manhattan, had opened up the rot in BCCI cesspit all on their own, Robert Morgenthau, Manhattan's District Attorney, told the world on Monday, 29 July 1991 of the 'largest bank fraud in world financial history'. The indictment spared no one. It accused the bank, its founder Abedi and former chief executive Naqvi, of swindling up to $20 billion from depositors around the world. 'The essence of the scheme was to convince depositors and other banking and financial institutions, by means of false pretences, representations and promises, that the BCCI group was a safe financial repository and institution for funds.'

Morgenthau said he wanted Abedi and Naqvi extradited to face the charges, which could mean prison terms of twenty-five years. The action called for a $200 million fine against BCCI and a permanent ban on any involvement with US banks by the men who had run or fronted the surreptitious takeover of First American: Agha Hasan Abedi, Swaleh Naqvi, Kamal Adham, the former head of Saudi Intelligence, Ghaith Pharaon, the Saudi financier, and five others – Hassan Kazmi, secretary of the ICIC Foundation, Faisal al-Fulaij, long-time chairman of Kuwait Airways, Abdul Raouf Khalil, a Saudi real estate investor, El-Sayed Jawhary, a passive investor in Financial General, and Khuaro Elley, a BCCI executive.

The document told of bribery, theft and false accounting. Abedi was pinpointed as primary felon. He was 'foremost among the originators of the scheme which was hatched on the day the bank was founded on 1 November 1972 until the day it was forcibly shut down on July 5 1991.' Morgenthau had no doubt that the intention to deceive was deliberate: 'The corporate structure of BCCI was set up to evade international and national banking laws so that its corrupt practices would be unsupervised and remain undiscovered. The defendants systematically falsified the capital structure of BCCI to make it appear as though it was a solvent, profitable bank secured by the backing of wealthy businessmen from the Middle East.

'In fact, much of the bank's capitalisation and assets were fictitious and its banking illusory. The defendants created the appearance of respectability by persuading world leaders to appear with them and defrauded their thousands of depositors, both small and large, who relied on that appearance of respectability,' said Morgenthau. This was gung-ho stuff, all that the Bank of England had feared, and the American response was nothing if not forthright.

Congressional and senatorial officials immediately found cover-ups and administrative cock-ups galore. Four separate special committees were formed to investigate what had happened, each with sweeping powers to summon and question witnesses. The first to start taking public, televised evidence was the Senate subcommittee on terrorism, narcotics and international communications, chaired by Senator John Kerry of Massachusetts. Kerry had an axe to grind, as he had originally followed up the behaviour of US Customs following the Tampa case in 1988. Jack Blum, counsel to the Senate Foreign Relations Committee back in 1988, took credit for the case going to Morgenthau in the first place, in 1989.

Jack Blum joined in the politicking in Washington that followed the New York indictment. He has consistently maintained that 'The Department of Justice had failed to act even though it consistently had evidence of wrong doing by the bank.' Blum was infuriated that the US prosecutors had concentrated on BCCI's money laundering and failed to follow up the financial chaos and malpractice that he had unearthed when he interviewed former BCCI treasury chief Syed Ziauddin Ali Akbar in 1988. Adding insult to injury, he was shocked by the 'outrageous decision' of the judge in the Tampa trial to give no more than a slap on the wrist to BCCI by allowing it to plea-bargain its way out of a full trial.

Blum 'concluded that they [the Department of Justice] weren't interested in or didn't have the capacity to go after these issues of capitalisation, or other illegal activities regarding the control of First American by BCCI. . . . I took the matter to Morgenthau in New York and told them I wanted an investigation into the capitalisation of BCCI and First American.'

Robert Morgenthau is made of sterner stuff than most of the American and British public prosecuting community. A bluff, no-nonsense performer, who had been Attorney General before falling out with his political masters, he came from a family of tough politicians and lawyers. He had made a name for himself in the high-profile 'wilding' case where a group of youths beat and raped a woman jogging in Central Park.

Following the indictments, and the blistering press assault on BCCI and all that sailed in her, the heat was turned on a number of public figures in the United States. Foremost among these was Clark Clifford, an icon of the Democratic party, but now eighty-five and rapidly losing the cloak of magisterial confidence that had so impressed presidents and judges alike. On 13 July he resigned as chairman of First American, together with his protégé Robert Altman, the bank's president. The case against them was that they had guided Abedi through the intricacies of US banking law at the time of the First American take-over.

Both men issued strenuous denials of any knowledge of BCCI's secret control of First American but, given the length of their connection with the bank as well as their history of close involvement with its affairs, the doubts grew rather than subsided. The two could certainly not argue that they were only advisers, given that both served on the board of BCCI companies, and they are thought to have made up to $18 million on share transactions connected with the group.

The British response to the showdown on Main Street was low-key to say the least. The Bank of England thought it had been rather brave to close down the bank, and now hoped that BCCI would go away. But the depositors were livid and the employees disgruntled. A political response was called for, and suggestions were made that Robin Leigh-Pemberton's head should roll. He had vigorously pooh-poohed the idea of any form of inquiry, but the Chancellor of the Exchequer was feeling the heat from Labour MP Keith Vaz, an Asian who had become the depositors' friend. Vaz was well suited to the legal fray; he had studied law at Cambridge University and although only thirty-four, had long battled for the Muslim cause. He had for example supported calls for the withdrawal of Salman Rushdie's novel, *The Satanic Verses*, while others said that smacked of censorship.

The Chancellor at last acceded to Vaz's demand for an inquiry into the supervision of BCCI. Shortly afterwards it was announced that Lord Justice Bingham would hear evidence in private. Depositors wanted something stronger, of course, but Prime Minister John Major reassured them that the inquiry would be very thorough, and that even he would not be allowed to escape questions about his role. This casual approach found few supporters, however. Mr Major seemed to miss the point that most people who had real evidence about the fraud would be unlikely to attend voluntarily.

Advertisements were placed in all newspapers appealing for witnesses to the crime:

## INQUIRY INTO THE SUPERVISION OF THE BANK OF CREDIT AND COMMERCE INTERNATIONAL

**THE RIGHT HONOURABLE**
**LORD JUSTICE BINGHAM**

Secretary
R. A. D. Jackson

Queen Anne's Chambers
28 Broadway
London
SW1H 9JS

1 August 1991

I have accepted an invitation extended to me by the Chancellor of the Exchequer on behalf of himself and the Governor of the Bank of England to undertake an Inquiry into the supervision of the Bank of Credit and Commerce International ('BCCI'). The Inquiry's terms of reference are: 'To inquire into the supervision of BCCI under the Banking Acts: to consider whether the action taken by all the UK authorities was appropriate and timely; and to make recommendations.'

The Inquiry will be carried out on behalf of the Treasury and the Bank of England. It will be non-statutory and the proceedings will take place in private. The results of the Inquiry will be made public subject to such restrictions as may be needed to avoid prejudicing any criminal proceedings and subject to the provisions of the Banking Act 1987.

The Inquiry is seeking assistance from the parties most directly involved in the supervision of BCCI but I am concerned to ensure that all reasonable lines of inquiry are pursued and to that end written submissions and evidence are invited from any party or member of the public with an interest in the subject matter of this Inquiry.

I must stress, however, that the Inquiry cannot deal with matters which relate to the Deposit Protection Scheme set up by the Banking Acts, or the recovery of deposits with BCCI generally, or other matters outside its terms of reference.

A statement of the procedure proposed to be followed during the Inquiry has been issued and a copy will be sent to all parties responding to this invitation.

The Rt Hon. Lord Justice Bingham

The Opposition Labour Party shadow chancellor, John Smith, made the most salient point. Commenting on the private nature of the inquiry he said: 'Labour will be drawing attention to the extraordinary contrast between the public nature of what is happening in the United States and the totally private nature of what is happening in this country.' Another Labour MP, Roy Hattersley, put the boot in, saying that UK depositors would learn more from the televised congressional hearings than they would from the Bingham inquiry.

The lobby protesting at the Bingham inquiry demanded the more formal Tribunal of Inquiry with its powers to order witnesses to attend. The one hope most have for Bingham is that the judge's own penetrating mind – and his reputation for asserting his independence – will make up for shortfalls in hard evidence. There were suggestions that Bingham was under pressure from the government to report early, no doubt in the hope of salvaging some Asian votes for the Tory party before the General Election. But Bingham was clearly having none of it. He made it clear that he was determined to speak to everyone, even if that meant travelling to Abu Dhabi, Hong Kong and Gibraltar. He would not be bulldozed by the US judicial process into an early and half-baked publication and he said it was inconceivable that he would be ready to report before the end of 1991 and that it would more likely be Easter or summer 1992.

The government took some steps to offset unhappiness with Bingham and the UK regulatory response to the BCCI closure with some vapid whistling in the wind. John Maples, the Economic Secretary to the Treasury, was full of confidence: 'I don't think the Bingham Report is going to find any fault on the part of the Treasury or the Bank.' With Bingham months away from a ruling that was hollow optimism.

Depositors would remain unhappy about Bingham and the degree of understanding of their case at the political level. The best they got from visits to the Chancellor of the Exchequer was 'tea and sympathy'. One grudge kept on coming up. As most of the depositors came from ethnic minorities, the issue got mixed up with race and discrimination in the financial sector. According to one campaigner, 'There is a large area of government which says it's a fringe bank, it's mainly for ethnic minorities. It's not a fringe bank, at the time of closure it was not a fringe bank, the Bank of England had prime responsibility as regulator. The informal inquiry was the least they could get away with.'

Low-key it might be, but Bingham's inquiry cannot be written off. The implications of a finding by the judge of maladministration by the Bank of England would prove disastrous for its Governor, Robin Leigh-Pemberton, who resisted the inquiry in the first place. Indeed, in money terms it could be serious for the UK Treasury. When the Department of Trade was found guilty of maladministration over its handling of the repeated warnings about Barlow Clowes, the depositors were paid out to the tune of 90 per cent. That was for a claim of $200 million.

BCCI is on a quite different scale. The Bank of England faces a possible exposure in the United Kingdom alone of $3.25 billion and that would be devastating for the Treasury. That would only be the start. There could be further claims in Europe against the Bank of England as it was seen as the principal regulator.

The United Kingdom's progress in arresting the perpetrators of the crime has been stumbling. It is known that the Serious Fraud Office (SFO) has taken a floor of City Gate House in Finsbury Square on the fringes of the City and that a deputy superintendent is in charge. But there is a widespread view that the best the British will net are some bit players. If angry depositors are to be placated, the SFO has no choice but to proceed. There was a brief flurry of activity when the SFO raided the offices of Capcom Financial Services, just a few doors down from its own headquarters in London's Gray's Inn Road. Shortly afterwards Syed Ziauddin Ali Akbar, the founder of Capcom, was arrested in Calais, but that was a joint operation with the French and outside British jurisdiction. The public relations effect of a dawn raid on the office of Nazmu Virani's Control Securities was lost when an SFO investigator was himself arrested. In short, the lot of the biggest team the SFO had ever assembled – twenty-two officers – was not a happy one.

The immediate effect around the world in the days and weeks following the closure of the bank can best be described as confused.

- In Sri Lanka they decided to reopen the bank, closed since 5 July, under the management of Seylan, one of the country's own banks.
- In the Seychelles they let the bank stay open just long enough to allow depositors to withdraw all their money, then they closed it, three days after everyone else.
- In Canada, Michael Mackenzie, superintendent of financial institutions, told a parliamentary committee in Ottawa that both he and the police authorities had closely monitored BCCI's operations for years and had found nothing untoward. He wished he had been kept better informed: 'We asked repeatedly – the police, the English, the Americans, the whole damn world – and nobody told us anything,' said Mackenzie with more than just a touch of pique.
- In Peru a special Senate committee was set up to look into the allegations made in the New York indictment that two former central bank officials, Hector Neyra and Leonel Figueroa, had taken $3 million in bribes in 1986. The finger was also being pointed at former president Alan Garcia, who just happened to be in the middle of an election comeback campaign.
- In Abu Dhabi meanwhile they were trying to get round some of the problems by changing the name of the bank from BCC Emirates to the Union National Bank.

There were also important diplomatic and political ramifications of the Bank of England's decision. At first the government of Abu Dhabi was so incensed by the abrupt shut-down in the United Kingdom that Sheikh Zayed let it be known that he had no intention of bail-ing out the bank's customers outside the Gulf region. Private depositors and businesses in the United Arab Emirates with an estimated $1 billion on deposit would be refunded.

Representing the majority shareholders, the Sheikh took out full-page newspaper advertisements outlining his displeasure. It is very unusual for any governments to communicate in this highly public way, but for the secretive and retiring Sheikh, it was quite extraordinary.

'The majority shareholders of the BCCI Group were shocked by the abrupt action taken by the Bank of England, the Luxembourg Monetary Institute and other regulators on Friday, 5 July 1991 to freeze the assets of the BCCI Group and close its operating branches. This action was taken without any consultation whatsoever with the shareholders of the Central Bank of the United Arab Emirates, a member of the College of Regulators. Since April 1990, the government of Abu Dhabi and related institutions have held a majority shareholding in the BCCI Group.'

It continued: 'The majority shareholders feel that they cannot absolve Price Waterhouse from all responsibility since they have been auditors of a major subsidiary [BCCI Overseas] for fifteen years and auditors of the whole group since 1987. . . .

'The action taken on 5 July has resulted in severe problems (involving financial hardship in many cases) for more than 1.25 million depositors of the Group worldwide and some 12,000 staff are likely to lose their jobs. It has resulted in the destruction, at a stroke, of what the majority shareholders believe was a well-structured and viable future plan. If the restructuring plan had been allowed to proceed, the majority shareholders have no doubt that no depositors' money would have been lost.

'In view of all the above, the majority shareholders deplore what they consider to be the unjustified action taken by the Bank of England, the Luxembourg Monetary Institute and other regulators on 5 July 1991.'

Robin Leigh-Pemberton did not need to wait for the advertisement to know the extent of the Sheikh's displeasure. He responded with courtesy, and visited the Ruler on his own territory. Leigh-Pemberton did more than merely build bridges, he also came cap in hand for yet more funds for the orderly winding-up of the bank. He personally delivered the damning Price Waterhouse report which until then the Sheikh and his advisers had not been allowed to see. There was talk at one stage of a minister being sent out to Abu Dhabi to add the Foreign Office's words of comfort, but that appeared to be abandoned when, according to some reports, the British ambassador to Abu Dhabi, Graham Burton, advised against it. The junior Foreign Office minister Douglas Hogg mended some bridges on a visit to the Gulf in October 1991.

The Abu Dhabi government felt it had been tricked into supporting the bank. It should have been informed and warned off. After all, the Sheikh was pumping millions of dollars into something which everyone knew would eventually have to be shut down, the final contribution having come just days before closure.

The Price Waterhouse report which the Governor delivered to Abu Dhabi would at first have made mystifying reading even for financial experts. The heading alone might have confused Sheikh Zayed:

## 'REPORT ON SANDSTORM SA UNDER SECTION 41 OF THE BANKING ACT 1987'

The covering letter and the report's forty-four pages are littered with elaborate code-names to baffle prying eyes – the copy the press was eventually allowed to read was doubly confusing as many of the crucial names were blacked out.

The gardening code words were eventually translated. Sandstorm equalled BCCI; Fork: ICIC; Tumbleweed: Faisal Islamic Bank; WXYZ: CCAH.

On the first page there is a disclaimer warning that the report is based on discussions with former members of management, that the information is incomplete and therefore 'the analyses of specific transactions given in this report should be treated with care'. Price Waterhouse add swiftly: 'It should be emphasised that much of the information contained in this report is based on records which have previously been concealed from us,' and in a taste of the fraudulent feast about to follow they write: 'The accounting records and financial position of the Group have been falsified in relation to the above transactions for a substantial number of years. In fact these transactions represent only a part of the wholesale deception to misrepresent and falsify the financial position of Sandstorm over the last decade through a series of complicated manipulations. These include the use of a related bank (Fork Overseas), which now appears to have been controlled by Sandstorm management; nominee and hold harmless arrangements with a substantial number of prominent Middle Eastern individuals.'

Price Waterhouse are in no doubt about the identities of the guilty parties in the whole affair: 'The strategic decisions to manipulate accounts and in particular how to make use of the ICIC relationship, the funds placed with ICIC, and the value within the shares of CCAH are those of Abedi and Naqvi.'

The report details the history of the bank and its particular banking techniques: the fraud, the nominee accounts, the elaborate holding companies and network of companies from Luxembourg to the United Kingdom and the Cayman Islands, to disguise transactions and the movement of funds. It points plainly to the fact that the use of ICIC (Overseas) was controlled by BCCI management.

It records the fraudulent use of deposits placed under the bank's management and outlines the regular use of unrecorded borrowings and agreements. Two sections of the bank's operation get special attention: the bad loans and the use of the treasury department in its failed bid to fill the gaping holes left by those loans.

The world of make-believe which the president and his chief executive tried to create when the non-performing loans of the Gokals' empire began to weigh heavily on the balance-sheet is summed up in one line: Abedi and Naqvi 'had to find a way of avoiding provisions on bad loans to Gulf, and also inflating the reported results to create the image of success'.

The report explains how the money was routed through banks and companies and how the success of the operation depended on collusion of major customers and falsifying information to the auditors. According to Price Waterhouse, life got so hectic that a 'special duties department' had to be set up. 'This was a full-time occupation which involved the manufacture of documentation, inflation of account turnover, concealment of funds, etc. and involved some 750 accounts over a fifteen-year period. Turnover in the period was over some $15 billion.'

In a follow-up letter to the Bank of England dated 4 July 1991, Price Waterhouse summed up their report as follows: 'We believe that the report reflects the general scale and complexity of the deception and falsification which have undoubtedly taken place over many years.'

Throughout the summer of 1991 there was still hope that a rescue package would be worked out. The depositors' champion, MP Keith Vaz, pressed on, spending the summer travelling to the key areas of Abu Dhabi, Hong Kong and Gibraltar, assessing the facts. The plea taken to Abu Dhabi was a simple one: Keep the bank alive.

'We met a couple of members of the royal family and the senior officials. Their prime hate target was the Bank of England. They said they had the press statement prepared announcing the establishment of the three new banks. It was the Bank of England who made them stop,' said Vaz. 'We felt there was a tremendous sense of betrayal. They had trusted the Bank of England. They had traded with the British for years and years. If the Bank of England had said jump they'd have jumped. If the Bank of England had said sack this person they would have sacked him. They wouldn't argue with the Bank of England. They had put an awful lot of money in BCCI and then to be cheated in this rather incredible way they found impossible to believe.' Vaz returned with a promise of $5 billion from Sheikh Zayed, sufficient to avoid immediate liquidation.

The controversy burned fiercely in Parliament. In July 1991 the question of who knew what and when became an opposition cudgel with which to beat the government over the head. Opposition leader Neil

Kinnock accused the Prime Minister of being 'utterly negligent' in his handling of the affair and of knowing of 'grave irregularities' in early 1990. For a moment John Major was speechless with rage. He stared straight at Kinnock and broke the Commons etiquette by not addressing his comments through the Speaker of the House when he replied, 'If you are saying I am a liar, you had better say so bluntly.'

Of course what no one could say was that a great many people in authority, presumably including the various Home Secretaries of the day, had known a great deal about BCCI many years earlier. Whether in his previous post as Chancellor of the Exchequer, Major had been privy to the precise details of BCCI's activities involving MI5, MI6, the CIA and the FBI, not to mention the French and Israeli security services, is not public knowledge.

It is, however, difficult to accept Robin Leigh-Pemberton's comments that there had been insufficient evidence of major fraud to enforce a shut-down before June 1991. He was treading through a potential minefield, of course. According to Qassem's account, the Bank of England was informed by MI5 that they had discovered all they needed in 1989. At that point their business was over and Operation Q – to close down BCCI – could begin. Individual cases then had to be looked into to establish a proper case against the bank which could be tested in court. MI5 officers clearly could not be called to tell everyone what they and their international comrades-in-arms had been up to for the past decade.

As the summer wore on, each day seemed to bring another dramatic revelation. The biggest billing in the newspapers and on television went to the 'revelations' of Masihur Rahman, BCCI's chief financial officer, who had resigned from the bank a year earlier. He said he had been forced to hide in London, fearing for his life as he and his young family had received death threats. Eventually he sent them to the United States where he later joined them to appear before the Kerry committee who treated him as the star prosecution witness in the trial of BCCI.

Rahman is the son of an Indian Chief Justice. At the time of writing he had not been implicated officially in any of the illegal activities. Nor had he been shot at. He joined BCCI in 1974 from the United Bank of Pakistan where he was one of the five founding members of the bank. He said he had been persuaded to join when Abedi spoke to him about his dream to build a Third World Bank which could be 'very useful socially and very profitable'. Despite his senior position in the bank he insists he was never part of the inner circle, although as chief financial officer he must have enjoyed a grandstand view of events.

After leaving BCCI he set himself up in business, establishing a trading company called Investment Management Associates International. Its location in London's St James's was prestigious but the office had none of the opulence to which he had become accustomed over the years at BCCI, nor could he enjoy the £120,000 a year salary he was used to in the good old days. By July 1991 business was effectively non-existent and Rahman said he depended on his friends to pay the bills. He now presents a desperate figure, looking older than his fifty-seven years, only his well-cut suit suggesting better times.

Before departing for the United States Rahman was anxious to tell his version of the story. But the bank gagged him before the closure with a High Court injunction supported by the provisional liquidators, Touche Ross, which restrained him from revealing bank secrets.

In the course of evidence to the Kerry committee Rahman pointed his accusing finger far and wide; first, there were lax management controls within the bank; second, there was incompetence by Price Waterhouse. He expressed shock that the staff benefit fund's 'golden nest egg' had been raided to plug the holes left by the bank's incompetent and fraudulent treasury which was dealing directly with the Cayman Islands and booking its transaction there – all this apparently under the unseeing eyes of the auditors.

'It was easy enough to meet the officers concerned and the Price Waterhouse team used to go and talk to them and see their accounts and books,' he said. It does seem a bit rich of Price Waterhouse to declare that the directors of BCCI 'have been taken in by, and trusted, the dominant and deceitful management'. Some might argue that Price Waterhouse themselves were more than just a little gullible.

And third, Masihur Rahman threw some arrows at the Bank of England. 'The Bank of England was grossly negligent,' he said.

Qassem's account of events and the involvement of the security forces may well explain why the Bank of England did not act more forcefully. There may also have been some pressure on Price Waterhouse to allow its various accounts to go through. But according to former colleagues of Rahman there is more than a whiff of 'He protesteth too much'.

Nadir Rahim, the former head of human resources, whose time with BCCI is comparable with Rahman's, said, 'Unfortunately Mr Rahman tends to shoot his mouth off. He was bitter because he definitely expected to be paid off to keep quiet.' Money was certainly high on Rahman's agenda in July 1991 when he and his London solicitor, Simon Gallant of Masons, said that the question of who he told his story to was down to money. Finally, in September, after appearing before the Kerry committee he again launched into an attack on Price Waterhouse and the Bank of England in the *Observer* newspaper.

Rahman expressed astonishment that Price Waterhouse had failed to detect the fraud for so long. But Price Waterhouse were working on the results of Rahman's own special four-man task force which was to produce its own 100-page report criticising the bank's conduct, and it was the less than frank answers Price Waterhouse were receiving which led to the hostile exchange of letters demanding more facts.

Rahman drew particular attention to the activities in the treasury department and the 'incompetence' with which he believed Price Waterhouse carried out their investigations and audits. He said it could not have been an easier audit to do, with all the people and the relevant files in the same room.

On 2 September 1991 Price Waterhouse could stand the accusations against them no longer and issued a statement saying that Rahman was 'aware of the facts but has misrepresented them'. Unfortunately at that stage they were prevented by the Banking Act from expanding on their statement.

Ghassan Qassem had no such qualms. He now regards himself as free to speak his mind. He said he employed Rahman's daughter – 'such a silly girl'. This was a fact Rahman conveniently overlooked when he later criticised Naqvi for employing his own relatives.

'That man was deeply involved in the restructuring of the balance-sheet, the fiddling and the cover-up. And suddenly he goes out in the open and says I did this and that,' said Qassem. Rahman's real motive for talking, Qassem believes, was because he did not get paid the compensation he wanted from the bank. Qassem continues. 'He was with the bank seventeen years. He was with Naqvi, with Saleem Sidiqi [in charge of inspection] the top policy-makers for seventeen years, and you tell me that that man was so stupid he didn't know what was going on?'

# 11 The Fleecing of the Innocents

The BCCI depositor's lot has not been a happy one since closure. The Muslim bank had a record of looking after the small man and his money exceptionally well, much better than the other banks in the high street. BCCI staff spoke many languages, understood small businesses' need for quick decisions, and made modest men feel cared for and affluent. This approach bore fruit, and Asian businessmen in particular, but people with international connections generally, joined the bank in their thousands. When the bank was closed these men received a major slap in the face. Many lost a substantial part of their savings and liquid assets, while politicians and the authorities did all they could to bury the problem, and these people's right to a hearing and fair compensation.

The depositors' one hope for a fair hearing rests on the Bingham inquiry, which was forced on the government almost singlehandedly by MP Keith Vaz. He won the initial battle to keep the bank alive and allow plans for a possible restructuring to be devised, but it was clear that he had lost the war when the Sheikh of Abu Dhabi announced that he was abandoning attempts to reconstruct the bank and to pay back depositors in full.

Vaz was fighting with a Bank of England which was determined to wrap up the whole business quickly and quietly with a High Court winding-up order. Sir Nicholas Browne-Wilkinson, Vice-Chancellor of the High Court, was not in such a rush when Gabriel Moss QC, for the Bank, put its case for immediate closure. Browne-Wilkinson was swayed by the government of Abu Dhabi's £50-million promise of interim payments to small depositors and employees of the bank, which he described as 'generous', and ordered a four-month stay of execution.

He noted that the Bank of England was 'not willing itself to contribute any cash' above the statutory maximum of £15,000 and he added that the Bank was 'putting undue stress on the English depositors at the expense of other creditors'. He ruled that he would not reconsider the question of a winding-up order until 2 December. This gave the 40,000 BCCI depositors in the United Kingdom something to hope for. Browne-Wilkinson was supported in his decision by the provisional liquidators, Touche Ross, whereas the Bank of England felt that this was giving depositors false hope.

The depositors were a mixture of large and small businessmen who were doubtless tempted by the bank's higher-than-average interest rates and took them at face value. Many of them will have understood the lessons of the Tampa conviction and have kept their accounts at £20,000 – the largest deposit qualifying for full 75 per cent repayment under the Bank of England's compensation scheme. Others who took advantage of BCCI's laundering facilities which they could not get at other banks were running a calculated risk. And of course others still will also have been borrowers, and are now sitting pretty on loans that may never have to be repaid . . . or at least not for a very long time.

But undoubtedly there is a large number of naive and certainly unlucky investors who thought a British bank was a safe place to park their funds. These people were to put their faith in a rescue by the Sheikh of Abu Dhabi or by the Bank of England, or anybody, but they would see their hopes so sadly dashed.

The story of Gulshan Loatey is typical. His small

import–export company, Upintan Ltd in Middlesex, traded mainly in leather for shoes and in allied machinery used in the tanning industry. He and his two colleagues prided themselves on maintaining a healthy balance-sheet. Together they had built up a modest business with a £1.5-million turnover.

Loatey's suppliers were in India and his main customers in continental Europe – Germany, France and Italy. The day before the closure of BCCI on 4 July, the bank's Leadenhall Street headquarters was instructed to pay DM93,000 to Loatey's supplier in India. The draft was made out and the cheques issued. Despite the date of the instruction, both have now been returned.

'The suppliers will go bust, we will go bust and the buyers are not going to wait for us. They will go to the competition and we are out of business,' said Loatey, whose business got hit twice. Priority is going to sterling customers and much of Upintan trade was in foreign currency.

Loatey is also typical of many of the BCCI victims in that he would still prefer to trade with the bank if a restructuring programme were agreed. He is not impressed with the 'shoddy work' of his new high street bank where they do not seem to be able to handle his international trade requirements.

'We used to go down to Leadenhall and talk to the people. We could sort everything out there. Give instructions there. They knew what was happening. I am still looking for a bank,' said Loatey.

Naresh Chada is managing director of Business Systems Computers International in Wokingham. His company exported computers to the Middle East, trading through a company in Sharjah in the United Arab

Emirates. It is a business he built up since returning from the United States in 1987. The company was launched the following year and in 1989 he opened his BCCI account. Once again, most of the transactions were in currencies other than sterling.

Chada was the middle-man in an increasingly competitive market. He would buy from a supplier and then resell to his customer. His last deal, in January 1991, involved a supplier from Germany. The trade was negotiated by BCCI in Deutschmarks. Chada decided to leave his payment in the German currency until the exchange rate improved. He had DM180,000 in his account – the equivalent of about £65,000. Chada cannot be accused of failing to read the papers or being unaware of the turmoil inside BCCI, a charge often thrown at BCCI customers.

'The irony is that in March one of their people came to see me. I took him out to lunch and talked about the problems and he said everything had been sorted out, you don't have to worry. The Sheikh has taken personal control and is trying to put the house in order. So that gave me a little reassurance to continue. Otherwise I could have withdrawn my Deutschmarks at that stage and closed the account,' said Chada.

Without a line in credit it seems certain that his business will fail. By September he had been forced to lay off three of his four staff. The business which he started with his own savings has stopped in its tracks.

'Now I don't have anything to put up front. My customers in the Middle East want the products. They won't wait. It won't take long before the business closes. We are talking weeks,' said Chada, who only expects repayment of the sterling balance in his account

– £135. He has already resigned himself to the loss of the Deutschmarks and $2,000.

He too has high praise for the BCCI staff he dealt with. They appreciated that delays in the paper work meant money lost. 'I don't think the bank cheated me at all. It is the Bank of England which has cheated me for not closing the bank earlier or making people aware of it,' said Chada, who with his young family of two daughters and a son now faces the prospect of having to start his business all over again.

One of the largest Muslim areas in the United Kingdom is in North West London. Asraf Hakim, a spokesman for the community, says he knows one retired BCCI officer who had his entire life savings with the bank, including his pension. The total amounted to more than £100,000. The man, a widower with a handicapped child, has had to move to be with his daughter in Sri Lanka. Without an income from his account, he risks becoming a burden on his daughter's family.

The North London Mosque inevitably turned to a Middle Eastern Bank for its needs. The mosque had £26–30,000 on deposit. It paid the wages of the Imam and the running costs. It depended on charity and all donations went straight into its BCCI account which is now frozen with little prospect of getting any of it back. Again, there is a strong feeling that somehow the customers were tricked by the authorities.

'The Sheikh was a sort of assurance to the people who deposited money with the bank,' said Hakim. 'Before he was involved, there was no proper base for the bank, but we felt happier when a country was involved.'

Hakim said the argument that people should have

known better cuts very little ice in his community. He says all the wrong-doing was known about by 1986 and his people cannot understand why it took until 1991 to close it down. Their anger is directed at the way it was closed, not at the bank itself. 'There was an atmosphere there, very homely. The people were very happy with the service the bank was providing.'

There are countless other tales of businesses which have failed or are threatened with closure. There is the freelance architect with three daughters from Shepherd's Bush in London. Now in his late fifties, he has worked all his life to save £50,000 towards his children's dowries to be given away on their wedding day. Today that means at least £15,000 plus another £5,000 for the wedding itself and anything up to £10,000 on gold and jewellery. All £50,000 had been deposited at BCCI's Luxembourg office. His daughters are now in their teens. Marriage cannot be far away. When the accountants and liquidators have finished their sums, the misery will continue.

Perhaps BCCI's best-known Asian client in the United Kingdom was Nazmu Virani, boss of Control Securities, the property and leisure group. Virani also happened to be one of BCCI's landlords at two of the bank's offices. He was putting a brave face on the news which came at the worst possible time in the middle of a major slump in property prices.

'We have fully provided against everything,' said Virani. He had in fact put £3.81 million aside in his end-of-year accounts to provide for losses – including non-payment of rent. Virani was not only BCCI's landlord. BCCI also owned 5.5 per cent of Control and he was also close to Ghaith Pharaon with whom he was joint owner of hotels in Spain. These deals later excited the suspicion of the UK's Serious Fraud Office who raided his offices in October 1991.

What befell the depositors in Spain and Gibraltar was one of the cruellest twists of the whole story, and because they are away from the spotlight they now feel forgotten. Along the Spanish coastline stretching from Gibraltar to Nerja – predominantly in the province of Malaga – five and a half thousand people anxiously read the papers and listen to the radio to hear the latest developments in the BCCI story. 98 per cent of them are British and most of them are pensioners. They moved abroad to enjoy their retirement in the sun. Many had sold up at home and bought well in Spain, taking advantage of the house price differences to put a little nest-egg away. Unfortunately the bank some of them chose was BCCI.

Overnight their combined savings worth £83 million were wiped out. They had their properties but by then the cost of living on the Costas had caught up with the British example, and so had the stagnant house market. Willy Shaw was lucky in that he only lost a small amount. He believes that puts him in a better position to act as chairman of the BCCI Gibraltar depositors group. He does not speak with bitterness in his heart, but that does not prevent him from being brought close to tears by the misery around him.

'It has affected many people very tragically. It has left a large number of people almost penniless. That's no exaggeration,' said Shaw. 'A man rang me and said his wife would probably die because he had money in the bank which paid for injections she had to have in England. I think they cost him about £1,000 including the flights. Now he can't pay because he has no money.

'At the other extreme I met a man who says he has three friends who between them have lost three quarters of a million pounds.'

The problem, as Shaw points out, is that there is no infrastructure, no DHSS to bail out the pensioners of Malaga. He flew to London and demanded a £23 million cheque from the Treasury to match the £5,000 per person the government was offering: at the very least he wanted something to pay immediate bills. The Treasury explained that there were banking law problems. The double irony is that BCCI in Gibraltar regularly forwarded its funds to London. Shaw estimates that there is £45–50 million of Gibraltar money frozen in the London vaults.

What if they do not get the money? 'I'm frightened to think, I really don't know what they are going to do. Most no doubt get a government pension which you could happily starve on in Spain. It is one of the lowest in Europe, if not the lowest, and the cost of living in Spain has shot up over the last few years.'

Shaw dismisses claims that people were just being greedy and going for the best interest rates. Shortly before the closure he said you could get a better price at other banks. But for many pensioners, the real attraction was the service BCCI provided and the low or non-existent charges on most accounts. 'Their general attitude towards the public was far better, far friendlier and far cheaper and more convenient than any of the other banks, and that really is the only reason why BCCI progressed so well on the coast,' said Shaw.

Early news to break following the closure was that many councils had banked with BCCI, apparently at the suggestion of money brokers R. P. Martin on the grounds that the bank paid higher interest rates. Of the fifty councils to have put money into BCCI, the biggest loser was the tiny Western Isles community in the remote Outer Hebrides off the Scottish Coast whose annual budget was less than £80 million. It had invested £23 million, mostly borrowed from institutions paying lower rates. With plenty of irony, it appears that the council's finance department, headed by Donald Macleod, had deposited the last £1.3 million fifteen minutes before the Bank of England moved. Macleod admitted, 'It's easy to say with hindsight we were wrong to put all our eggs in one basket.'

The Western Isles and other councils at the time argued that BCCI was on a Department of the Environment list of financial institutions; BCCI was already being investigated for fraud when that list was issued. The Bank of England countered that it was just a legal formality listing banks which had been issued with a licence to take deposits. In fact the list was so unreliable that a recent list included two organisations which had already gone into administration – Chancery and Edington.

Deciding who should carry the can in the Western Isles was as muddled as their financial philosophy. At first Macleod stepped down, only to be reinstated when the convener (the chairman), the Rev. Donald Macaulay, resigned 'as a matter of honour' – although he said he had had nothing to do with the investment. Meanwhile, the council wasted no time in applying for another government grant of £23 million to cover the loss.

BCCI turned the spotlight on the qualifications of council treasurers, and how they came to invest without the knowledge regarding BCCI that was current in the

City. York City Council, which invested £1.3 million with the bank, seemed to have an unquestioning faith in their brokers. 'We phoned up the brokers saying how much we had to invest. They came back and said, "I can place it with BCCI at a rate." We said, "Is it on the Bank of England list?" They said, "Yes." That was sufficient, they don't tend to come up with a range of options,' said a spokesman.

The brokers themselves passed the buck on to the Bank of England. They quoted the Bank's own rules and regulations on the subject from its Grey Paper which is properly if longwindedly called 'The Regulation of the Wholesale Markets in Sterling, Foreign Exchange and Bullion'. This states: 'Principals are reminded that the ultimate responsibility to assess the creditworthiness of a counterparty [bank], whether or not it is supervised, rests with them, whether or not the deal is done directly or through a broker.' In other words, the councils must carry the can and they in turn will need to put up their poll taxes to make up the deficit.

The Prime Minister, John Major, was pressed to help the councils out, but he turned a deaf ear. In answer to one Labour MP he said that the risks of an investment in the bank should have been obvious to the council treasurers, some of whom are said to earn as much as £70,000. 'Any accountant or finance officer should know that if an institution pays over the market rate of interest, it is in the form of a risk premium. Local authorities have a duty of care over the funds entrusted to them. That implies taking a prudent view of risk, and spreading risk.'

One side-effect of the loss of confidence in the smaller banks was the so-called 'flight to quality'. There were real fears that depositors would abandon the secondary banking sector and starve it of cash. A number of councils effectively ruled out placing deposits with anything other than the main UK clearing banks or the top twenty building societies. The Association of District Councils estimates that its members have approximately £8 billion with banks, and half of this would be with the second and third league institutions; they began to feel the squeeze almost at once.

This time the Bank of England stepped in quickly and exerted behind-the-scenes pressure on the high street banks and the City for some of the 'windfall' deposits to be passed on to the smaller firms. A spokesman of the Bank was quoted as saying: 'We can well understand that some local authorities would be nervous in the wake of the BCCI affair but that should be seen as an exceptional case. We would not expect local authority treasurers to react in an indiscriminate way or one which might prejudice their own interests.'

The salvage operation continued around the world – it seems every leading lawyer, fraud and insolvency expert was employed in some courtroom on the BCCI case. In the secretive Caymans, the Abu Dhabi government wanted to delay attempts to wind up the operation and appealed against the revocation of banking licences for BCCI (Overseas) and Credit and Finance Corporation (CFC). The more infamous part of the empire, International Credit and Investment Company (ICIC) was let go.

Wherever a new operation was proposed, a prerequisite had to be entirely new management throughout. In Abu Dhabi itself a committee was set up to consider a relaunch chaired by Sheikh Zayed's son Mohammed, Ghanim al-Mazrui, the head of the

Sheikh's private department, and Yousef Omeir bin Yousef, the oil minister.

In Gibraltar officials were desperately trying to get the pensioners included in any hand-out. Hopes that they too might benefit from any help coming from Abu Dhabi were fading. On his fact-finding mission Keith Vaz stumbled on an over-eager provisional liquidator who had put two of the local branches up for sale. 'We stopped him because we thought that would be very damaging indeed,' said Vaz, who was keen to keep as much of the old bank alive as possible.

Depositors were not so lucky in Canada where Justice Perry Meyer authorised the formal appointment of a liquidator after the Abu Dhabi government's attorney said his client was no longer prepared to offer a separate settlement for BCCI Canada. It was to be the first liquidation of the bank.

For the 40,000 UK-based depositors, the news they had least wanted arrived on 3 October 1991 when Abu Dhabi announced that there would be no rescue after all. Over a thousand jobs would go and a mere handful of staff kept on just to 'manage away' the assets. The announcement followed news of 300 job losses in Abu Dhabi itself. The corpse of the Bank of Credit and Commerce International was being disposed of.

There seemed to be a note of grim satisfaction from the Bank of England in its terse statement noting the Sheikh of Abu Dhabi's decision; more or less 'Well, we told you so.' As far as the Bank was concerned, the orderly winding-up it had sought earlier would begin on 2 December. That would allow the depositors to claim up to 75 per cent of their deposits, up to a maximum of £15,000 from the Government's Depositors' Protection Scheme. But the statement left some room for hope for creditors in other parts of the world – the bank operated in more than seventy countries. There was the implied suggestion that something could still be worked out, if branches were sold as a going concern.

The depositors were stunned. Chan Chowdry, a North London businessman who had seen close friends lose 'literally thousands' spoke for many when he said: 'People had hoped to get something out of it and now the reality has proved to be the worst of all. Everything is lost. They are sure the Bank of England didn't make an attempt to help. They made no effort at all.' They felt they had been betrayed. According to Chowdry many felt certain a package would be worked out once the Sheikh had intervened and the ring-leaders were rounded up. 'They feel they have been led up the garden path,' said Chowdry.

Mohammed Anwar, who ran an international shipping agency and electrical outlet in Manchester, could not quite believe it had happened. 'I'm totally shattered; we were hoping Abu Dhabi would help us out. Sixteen years of hard work has just gone down the drain.'

But all was not yet lost in the eyes of the depositors in Spain and Gibraltar who, while shocked, still clung to the fact that the United Kingdom appeared to have been singled out in the Abu Dhabi announcement. Clutching at straws, perhaps, the pensioners are still counting on a restructuring of their banks. 'Whatever happens in England, we don't count ourselves part of it because he has not specified Gibraltar or any other country,' said Willy Shaw. Speculating on the Sheikh's real motives he added, 'It's possible that this is his reaction to the British government's attitude towards Abu

Dhabi.' Shaw said there was still time to mend fences and his group were considering a visit to Abu Dhabi.

While they awaited exact news of their fate, normal life was becoming increasingly desperate. Mike Parkhurst is a former company director who now, at the age of fifty, has started work as a waiter for 500 pesetas an hour at a restaurant in the tiny village of Mijas inland from Torremolinos. He had taken advantage of the property market, sold a house in Spain and a home in the United Kingdom, and banked £400,000 with BCCI in Gibraltar. Just a few days before the closure he had signed a contract to buy a new home. With no depositors' protection scheme to help out, he says his only chance of recouping some of his money rests with the Sheikh of Abu Dhabi. 'What we are hoping is that for those outside Britain there might still be some form of restructuring or rescue package,' said Parkhurst. 'We are now homeless, cashless and we've got furniture in store in the UK and furniture in storage in Spain.'

To the dismay of Keith Vaz, the campaign leader, he was forced to tell the depositors that the campaign was effectively over, the only hope of recouping more was if the Bingham inquiry found negligence and recommended compensation. The depositors were after blood, according to Vaz, who was shocked that the Sheikh had decided against a reconstruction plan after so much effort had gone into studying the possibilities of a reconstruction. He was beginning to suspect some other motives. 'There is something going on we don't know about,' said Vaz. 'What were all those officials doing in Abu Dhabi?'

While he still clung to the hope that something could be saved in other parts of the world, Vaz's anger was now directed at what he saw as the slow progress of the

Bingham inquiry; many families who had seen their life savings disappear into BCCI's elegant portals would have to wait months for possible compensation. He said that the Treasury had refused to put any pressure on Bingham to speed things up. 'It's going to be too late – June next year is too long.'

For many of the UK bank employees there would be the double shock of losing their jobs and their homes. Most of them had loans in the form of mortgages still outstanding. The total was estimated at £49 million. The debt would be collected from their redundancy cheques and they were given three months to repay the balance, but with a banking career in BCCI the prospects of a new job looked slight. As Richard Lynch of the Banking, Insurance and Finance Union said, 'A reference from BCCI is almost worthless. There are large numbers of job losses in financial services and some workers may become almost unemployable in banking.'

# 12 Regulators Cop Out

When BCCI closed there was a rush for scapegoats. Some depositors argued that if the fraud was so serious it should have been discovered earlier and then they would never have invested. Others said it could have been solved with a little help from the Sheikh of Abu Dhabi, and that the supervisors had acted rashly. Clearly, no one was going to be happy.

The appointment of Lord Justice Bingham to head a not-so-public inquiry to consider whether the Bank of England's action was 'appropriate and timely' may take some of the steam out of these criticisms. But many feel that there is no need to wait for the Bingham Report, and having already decided that it was neither appropriate nor timely, are now calling for tougher controls. There might, however, be a risk of leaping from one extreme to the other.

Dr Max Hall, lecturer in economics at Loughborough University in England, said, 'The biggest danger is over-reacting to what may be a unique situation.' Nevertheless, what he described as 'the abysmal attempt' to date in trying to detect fraud has to be addressed, as most bank failures result precisely from fraud and not from a lack of capital.

Banking regulation in the United Kingdom is dominated by the 1987 Banking Act which became law soon after the collapse of the Johnson Matthey Bank in October 1984. It was acknowledged later that the Bank of England did not pick up the problems at JMB soon enough. Despite that experience, many argue that the Bank of England was slow in moving against BCCI too. In retrospect it seemed that the Bank would be blamed either way, whether it closed BCCI too soon, or left it to go further on its fraudulent way.

It had been widely known in financial circles for many years that BCCI was at the very least an unsound base for deposits. So that by the end not a single major international bank (with the possible exception of American Express who had deposited $30 million) suffered from a large exposure. The Bank of England would insist that it had not yet got the hard information. 'There was a lot of talk about this bank and it was rumour and it was suspicion, maybe, but certainly not information on which the Bank of England could necessarily act,' Robin Leigh-Pemberton told the House of Commons committee.

There are those who argue that the Bank of England's eventual actions were determined by political and security considerations. But even if one accepts that it was acting on strictly banking criteria, the Governor, having left it so long, was now on the spot, with the American investigation hounding him. Once the decision had been taken to act, it had to be implemented instantly. As Garth Hewitt of *Banking World* put it, 'There is no such thing as a little pregnancy and there is no such thing in banking as a little warning.' The slightest whiff that the bank was regarded as a liability and there would have been a run on it, with more chaotic consequences.

The Bank of England decided to hold off from using what it called the 'nuclear option' at first, relying on the college of regulators to take control in the hope of keeping the bank as a going concern. BCCI was not the first instance of fraud the Bank of England had encountered and, according to Robin Leigh-Pemberton, 'Our experience in the past is on the whole that we have been able to correct that sort of thing by the dismissal of management and closer supervision.'

But supervising BCCI had never been easy. Its founders devised a structure to confuse. BCCI was a stateless bank with no prime regulator. Its headquarters were in Luxembourg, it had a major bank in Grand Cayman, its centre of operations was in London and its main shareholders were in Abu Dhabi. By slipping between the crevices of international regulation BCCI has been a débâcle for the world's leading banking supervisors. Belatedly they are learning some of the lessons.

In Luxembourg, for example, banking authorities do not scrutinise holding companies as they are not considered to be banks. The Grand Duchy now wants to plug that gap. Pierre Jaans of the LMI has called for the law to be changed so that any banking group would be barred from establishing its headquarters in the Grand Duchy through a holding company, if its main operations are in other countries. BCCI was something of a unique case in Luxembourg where none of the other 180 banks, with total assets of $350 billion, had a similar structure. But that has not stopped the banking fraternity from raising their voices in alarm about tougher regulations in relation to drugs trafficking and the possible threat to their prized banking secrecy laws. The Duchy's banking association was particularly worried about the threat of criminal proceedings not only against those who had knowingly committed an offence but also against those who 'by failing to appreciate their professional obligations have contributed to any operation of placing, concealment or conversion of the proceeds of an infringement of the legislation regulating the sale of drugs'.

From the United States there has been a call for a more unified approach towards regulating banks operating across national boundaries. With commendable prescience, the Group of Thirty, a Washington-based Think Tank, wrote just before the BCCI closure of the difficulties of supervising banks which have branches in many countries. It recommended that foreign operations should either be regulated as extensions of their domestic business when they would be subject to home country control or should be treated as local banks and subject to the host country's regulations.

A report from the House of Representatives' judiciary sub-committee regarding 'federal law enforcement's handling of allegations involving BCCI', which was published in early September of 1991, indicates areas where the government failed to act. The sub-committee, which had interviewed officials from the Internal Revenue Service, the US Customs, the drug enforcement administration and the Department of Justice, says that as early as 1983 incidents had come to light in which criminals were using BCCI 'as a conduit', or where the bank itself was an 'active participant in possibly criminal activity'. The report goes on, 'The government simply overlooked the repeated run-ins that it had with BCCI, its officials, customers and accounts. Any reasonable review of those historic files would have led a knowledgeable investigator to BCCI far earlier. Perhaps it would have uncovered sooner the staggering international proportions of BCCI's illicit business, and put it out of business.'

The sub-committee says that one arm of US law enforcement did not know what the other was doing. It states, for example, that Operation C-Chase, which netted the four BCCI bankers after the Tampa sting, was prematurely stopped because US Customs officials 'failed to ensure that adequate resources were available to prosecute the bank to the fullest extent of the law. . . . Although prosecutors finally succeeded in winning $15 million in forfeitures and convictions against all individuals, more attention should have been given to levelling federal racketeering charges.' The agent involved in C-Chase, Robert Musella, has also alleged it was stopped prematurely.

The sub-committee also unearthed fifteen cases emanating from BCCI which had gone before the Internal Revenue Service (IRS), and ten are due for prosecution. But, incredibly, 'no one at the agency appeared to have noticed the pattern. Most startling of these is the refusal of top management officials at IRS on three separate occasions in 1986 to begin an undercover operation of BCCI at the request of a South Florida agent who had information on BCCI from a former employee.'

Senator John Kerry, the Democratic party's scourge of BCCI, must also have been looking in his legislative crystal ball. He was pushing for tougher measures to combat drug money laundering but was regarded as something of a nuisance on Capitol Hill. The moment BCCI closed, legislators began pushing a Foreign Banking Supervision Enhancement Act through Congress.

Things moved at a more leisurely pace in the United Kingdom. John Maples, the Economic Secretary to the Treasury, told Parliament that the government had ruled out any immediate increase in the Bank of England's regulatory powers, but he observed that the Bank would be reflecting on any lessons the BCCI case held for future regulation.

The creation of Europe's single market in 1992 might actually make matters worse for banking supervision. Under the EC's second banking directive which is due to take effect on 1 January 1993, the home country will have to assume greater responsibility for assuring the safety of its own banks.

At present the only degree of coordination is based on the gentlemen's agreement of the Basle Concordat between the G10 – group of ten industrialised nations. The Concordat allocates responsibilities between parent and host supervisory authorities, with everyone policing their own little corner. Its influence is limited precisely because it is nothing more than a gentlemen's agreement and one without teeth. Whatever is to be done will cost money, and the larger clearing banks who claim to have adequate supervision in place will be reluctant to subsidise the less well-managed operations.

When he announced the indictments against BCCI on 29 July 1991, Robert Morgenthau left no doubt about the problems facing the world's banking regulators: 'We have much yet to discover about this bank, and much to do in reforming international banking practices. The key to the scheme was that BCCI was structured in such a way that no single central bank was able to monitor its activities. No foreign bank should be permitted to operate in the United States unless it is supervised by a single, strong, central bank and is not bound by bank secrecy laws of another jurisdiction. Without these reforms the potential for massive worldwide bank fraud remains.'

If the supervisors were not able to supervise, what were the auditors doing? Price Waterhouse need to be singled out for criticism for not blowing the whistle sooner. Their defence is two-fold. First, they shared the auditing responsibilities with Ernst and Whinney and only assumed total control towards the end of 1987, and second, auditors are not there to investigate.

The first line of defence, that there were two auditors, sounds a little hollow when Price Waterhouse had prime responsibility for the Cayman operation where much of the funny business took place and where some tougher questions might have been asked. The second is increasingly becoming a vital management issue. The big five accountancy firms who check the books are increasingly beset with conflicts of interest. On the one hand they have auditing departments which give the certificate declaring the accounts to be true and fair, and on the other they have management consultancy arms who carry out everything from company reorganisations to head-hunting top staff. Keeping the two apart is not just problematic, but must raise questions about whistle-blowing and propriety. For example, it was Price Waterhouse who set up BCCI's new treasury operation in Abu Dhabi and appointed some of the staff on behalf of the authorities there. Price Waterhouse make much of the traditonal role, claiming that people misunderstand the job of the auditor which is to check that the papers are there rather than to investigate.

In law auditors strictly speaking only owe a duty to members of the company and not to anyone else. Solicitors acting for the depositors advised their clients against taking an action against Price Waterhouse for that reason. It has also been established that auditors do not owe a duty to prospective purchasers of shares under the legal dictum of 'You cannot extend a tort to an innominate class of people in an undefined amount.' Auditors are required to form an opinion as to whether a set of accounts is true and fair, and even if they stumble across fraud they are not obliged to report it to the regulators, although under the Banking Act they have a right to do so if they feel so inclined. Above all, auditors have a duty of confidentiality to their clients, which must only be broken if they uncover treason or terrorist offences relating to Northern Ireland.

For Ian Brindle, who became senior partner at Price Waterhouse five days before the scandal broke, BCCI was something of a baptism of fire. Brindle hammered home the difficulties his firm faced when it came to signing off the accounts in 1987, 1988 and 1989. There could be no half-measures, he said. 'You simply can't go around qualifying the accounts of a bank without creating all sorts of problems, without the whole thing collapsing,' he said. There is frustration in the Price Waterhouse camp as owing to their duty of confidentiality to the Bank of England they say they are unable to answer back to some of the criticisms. Unofficially they say there was a sense of accomplishment that they managed to get to the bottom of what had been happening since they took full charge of the books so quickly.

Was there a degree of naivety about the way Price Waterhouse went about their business? Jahangir Masud, an investment banker who knew the bank well, told the British TV Channel Four programme, 'The Bandung File', that they were easily misled. On one occasion they wanted to look at the books relating to the BCCI affiliate KIFCO (the Kuwait International Finance Company), which was being audited by a local Kuwaiti firm.

'Price Waterhouse were told that under Kuwaiti law they could not visit Kuwait to examine the books of KIFCO to carry out their own investigations,' said

Masud. They happily went along with this until they checked with the Central Bank of Kuwait and the Ministry of Finance who said there was no such law.

According to Masud, the internal auditors were 'not allowed anywhere near the treasury', which was the source of one of the bank's major losses, or into the department handling loans to insiders or shareholders of BCCI. Despite that, the alarm bells never rang in the Price Waterhouse ears.

Masud said that preparations for Price Waterhouse's arrival at BCCI every year were quite intense: 'Mr Naqvi headed a committee of senior executives that would decide what to tell Price Waterhouse, what not to say to them, what management analyses to present and what files were to be presented.' Nevertheless, far from being kept secret, many of the files were openly available to the auditors. Masud said the famous 'Naqvi files' were in fact available throughout the bank at Leadenhall Street and in a neighbouring building, Cunard House.

What Bingham's examination will decide is whether the rules or the regulations are more to blame for the BCCI fiasco. Some will also argue that BCCI was a beneficiary of the ethos of banking self-regulation in the UK. In that case, the whole system may have learnt a lesson.

# 13 Fiddles Galore!

Fraud is endemic in banking. Most of it happens at a low level and can be cut out like a malignant tumour. BCCI, however, was not just a few bad cells, but a cancerous body scarred by money laundering and arms financing, as well as more superficial wounds like foreign exchange cheating, capital flight and share-ramping. BCCI was infecting the banking population as a whole and had to be cut out *en masse*. No one imagines that that has reduced the total amount of fraud in the system, and perhaps the most interesting question is the whereabouts of the laundered accounts and the crooks who were given access to BCCI.

That said, the BCCI fraud has topped the bill for stolen bucks. Estimates abound. They start at $5 billion and go up to $15 billion. But from whom did the money come, what happened to it in the middle, and to whom did it go? The money came from two sources, share-holders and depositors. BCCI took billions from the Arab sheikhs and gave them worthless shares. Deposi-tors' funds were raided to the tune of billions to satisfy the shareholders' need for dividends and the investors' need for interest. The money went to people who took out tens of millions of dollars-worth of commercial loans without any intention of paying the loans back. But equally there were employees who were paid millions to keep quiet, middle-men in the Third World who creamed a percentage out of BCCI's loans, and fraudulent staff who dealt on their own account with the bank's money.

Robert Morgenthau described what the bank was doing as a 'Ponzi scheme'. This is named after an Italian fraudster of the 1920s who obtained a loan from one bank, then went to a second bank to get another loan, which he used to pay off the interest on the first loan. That kept his creditors satisfied for a foray against a third bank. Said Morgenthau: 'The essence of the scheme was to convince depositors and other banking and financial institutions by means of false pretences, representations and promises that the BCCI group was a safe financial repository and institution for funds.' That required inflating the bank's shareholdings and its capital. The bank was able to use its stock and the stock of its multiple subsidiaries so freely for two reasons. First, because fraudulent insiders controlled the bank virtually from top to bottom. Second, BCCI had the advantage of a large number of available nominees at its disposal, who either knew what was going on, and were happy to be bribed, or didn't know, and allowed themselves to be duped. Fraud perpetrated by an insider is always more dangerous than that conducted by somebody outside. But when the fraud is run by the men at the top of a bank, with straw men, anything is possible. Add to this the likelihood that some of BCCI's largest customers were in collusion with the bank and there is no chance of detection before big damage has been done.

Fixing the books was a way of life at BCCI, but this degree of abuse needed massive decoration of accounts to escape detection. BCCI had no compunction about getting into bed with people it knew wanted to use the bank for criminal purposes, if they brought in more funds. It is a heady cocktail of fraud, never before seen under one roof.

BCCI needed to inflate its shareholders' capital to offset the effect of the loans to outsiders that never got paid back. It did this by issuing shares from one company, and paying someone to buy them with money from another. It was an ingenious form of kiting, where less and less money kept more and more shares flying ever higher. As the holes in the bank's books got bigger, the bank's directors went to any lengths to find capital. Anyone with money was drawn into BCCI, and anyone who knew anyone with money got larger and larger commissions. This money-go-round could only end in disaster.

The bad-loan book also meant BCCI had to cook its profits. A bank cannot go on lending indefinitely, unless it is showing that the business is profitable. But as early as the late 1970s BCCI reached the point where calling in bad loans would have been more dangerous than making accountants believe they were still good. It had to pretend that the loan would be repaid in order to charge interest and count the loan as an asset of the company. As soon as the bank says it will not be repaid, it must be written off as a loss. BCCI decided to pretend the huge loans would still be repaid, to give the appearance of solvency.

Creative accounting to deceive auditors and shareholders is one thing, giving regulators the run-around is another. BCCI's hijacking of Financial General from under the regulators' noses with secret offshore companies may yet be seen as the fraud that broke BCCI. It was a foreign bank with dubious shareholders, and the rule-makers in Washington and New York did not like it. So BCCI put up a veil between its own shareholders and those of an offshore company, called Credit and Commerce American Holdings (CCAH), registered in the Netherlands Antilles. It worked because apparently respectable people argued its case.

Offshore finance is mostly used to dodge the taxman. Lawyers saw no difference in using an offshore company to dodge regulators. The island havens protect investors with ill-gotten gains from the prying eyes of overseas tax investigators, but that secrecy can equally extend to details about shareholdings and control. In fact the Netherlands Antilles enable shareholders to be especially opaque. Ingo Walter in his book *Secret Money* writes: 'It appears that the Netherlands Antilles serve as a transfer point rather than a collection point. By the time the money flows through a Netherlands Antilles Corporation, the real owners of the funds are so well screened by local Antillean nominees and agents that it is virtually impossible to identify them.' The Netherlands Antilles might cooperate with US investigations into US citizens, but foreigners are safe, and that makes it difficult to investigate complex cash flows.

BCCI needed many offshore companies to hide its financial statements and lists of real shareholders. Companies like this can be acquired for $1,000 or so, with minimal disclosures about finances or proof of directors' identity. BCCI's main offshore haven was the Cayman Islands. BCCI Cayman, composed of its web of ICIC companies and trusts, served as a booking unit for BCCI's non-performing loans around the world. According to a report from accountants Deloitte Ross Tohmatsu who are overseeing the bank's affairs on the islands, BCCI Cayman had $3.3 billion in loans booked at the end and $2.2 billion outstanding to ten unidentified Middle East entities. More than half of the bank's $753 million deposits were also from related BCCI entities. The accountants are currently investigating the activities of the BCCI Cayman companies, trusts and foundations which formed the ICIC group.

Cayman is a British Crown Colony with a reputation among offshore centres for tight regulation. Two hundred and twenty billion dollars-worth of deposits are estimated to be held in some 450 Cayman banks and trust companies. Cayman companies must have a registered office there, a name-plate on the door, and hold an annual shareholders meeting. They do not have to file accounts or be audited. When the BCCI scandal broke, the Caymans' banking inspector said that the islands were only used as an administrative centre, and the 'decisions were taken elsewhere'.

BCCI was not just built on secrecy and deception, but it also sold them as an essential part of its banking service. Crooks with ill-gotten gains came to the bank to have them secretly laundered. This was lucrative business, and the more illicit the funds, the more complex the hiding operation, and the more the bank can charge. BCCI was always expensive, but when it came to hiding dictators' ill-gotten gains, it charged top dollar.

When the bank was caught laundering Panamanian drug money through its Tampa offices, the word was out. BCCI was not merely fiddling the books or using a few offshore fiddles, but aiding the worldwide drugs traffic. The figures from laundering drugs money are vast and the profit potential considerable. Three years ago it was estimated that sales of drugs in the United States were in the order of $100 billion. Around a fifth of that will have gone abroad to pay expenses, including of course paying the original producers. Of the remaining $80 billion, half is thought to be invested in property or financial instruments abroad, and half stayed in the United States for investment in legitimate business. Worldwide law enforcement authorities have decided that stopping the money getting into the banking system is top priority, and BCCI paid for it at the Tampa trial, where it was convicted of money laundering.

In fact, BCCI has a history of brushes with the law. It has been accused of breaking foreign exchange controls – in effect, smuggling currency – in six Third World countries. The bank was found guilty in Mauritius in 1983, and in Colombia in 1989. In the Colombia case, BCCI was found guilty of a series of currency and administrative irregularities and fined the equivalent of $11,000. In Brazil, the president of BCCI's subsidiary was stopped by police at São Paulo airport and accused of trying to smuggle $150,000-worth of traveller's cheques to Paraguay. Those charges were dropped. In 1990 several bank officials were convicted in Florida of failing to report large cash transactions for Latin American drug dealers.

In most of these cases the charges were related to foreign exchange controls, which BCCI broke with abandon. But here they were doing nothing more than institutionalising what Indians and Pakistanis have been doing for decades, namely, passing money across the world using an underground banking system which worked on trust and close family networks.

This is called the Hundi or Hawalla banking system and BCCI operated it for the many thousands of Asians around the world who used it to bypass Indian and Pakistani exchange controls and UK Inland Revenue observation. It was no accident that BCCI set up branches in many cities where Pakistani migrant workers would have use of a formal banking Hundi system. Using Hundi banking, an agent in one city takes a client's cash and then authorises his counterpart in another city, usually a relative or loyal friend, to release cash to someone on behalf of the client.

The system rode on the back of a mass movement of Pakistanis from their home country to construction jobs in the Gulf. Of course this was perfect for BCCI, which was well represented in both places. Between 1978 and 1987 more than one million Pakistanis worked overseas, and in 1983 official published remittances, let alone those that slipped through the net, were $2.9 billion.

BCCI also ran a Hundi system for Nigerians, which cost Nigeria's Exchequer some $200 million. Foreign exchange rules are tight in Nigeria, albeit rarely observed. Exports of foreign exchange and letters of credit are controlled by the Nigerian central bank, but the central bank takes some six months to process requests. In a lead article in the *Financial Times* of 16 September 1991, it was stated, 'Because of the delay in processing the foreign exchange, BCCI would ask both the Nigerian importer and the foreign exporter without the knowledge of the other, for interest payments on the money advanced on the purchase during the waiting period . . . the fraud depended on the ability of BCCI to conceal from the Nigerian authorities that it was charging interest twice over on the same letter of credit.'

For some, the growing evidence of its deceptive takeover of Financial General was BCCI's Rubicon, because it indicated that the bank was not merely ripping off the Third World, but was now cheating the US banking system as well. Others see the Tampa conviction as crucial. But it had been known that the bank had laundered cash for many years in South America, and certainly the bank's shareholders had been no secret to some journalists for many years, so it is certain that the banking authorities knew.

So why did it take so long for the authorities to act? The answer to that $15 billion question will likely never be known. It may have little to do with BCCI's transgressions of banking law, which were no worse than those of many banks in much better-regulated environments, but much more to do with the fact that BCCI was used by security services both to pay off undercover staff and to monitor the money and movements of wanted men, especially terrorists. They will have exercised great surreptitious pressure on the bankers to keep the cancerous body alive long past the day when prudent bankers acting independently would have turned off its life-support machine.

# Epilogue

As BCCI's investigators dig deeper, they are not only finding more evidence of fraud, but indications of commercial involvement between the bank and figures at the heart of the American political system. These are bound to stimulate the current debate about the length of time it took the global banking regulators to close down BCCI. It also appears that obstacles are being placed in the path of the investigators which may prevent the full story eventually being unearthed.

BCCI's role in assisting the US to fund Mujaheddin guerrillas in Afghanistan fighting the Soviet occupation is drawing increasing attention. The bank's role began to surface in the mid-1980s when stories appeared in the *New York Times* showing how American security operatives used Oman as a staging post for Arab funds. This was confirmed in the *Wall Street Journal* of 23 October 1991 which quotes a member of the late General Zia's cabinet as saying 'It was Arab money that was pouring through BCCI.' The bank which carried the money on from Oman to Pakistan and into Afghanistan was National Bank of Oman where BCCI owned 29 per cent. The Mujaheddin connection is being pursued by US investigators who are examining a company called International Six which was founded by Omar Zawawi, the personal adviser to the Sultan of Oman. International Six's vice president was Brent Scowcroft, the national security adviser to President Bush. Other members of International Six have been military experts attached to various US presidents. International Six ceased to function after 1988.

Kamal Adham, the BCCI investor and front man, is

claiming to have new information about the connection between BCCI, the White House, and the Mujaheddin which he is threatening to reveal unless the American BCCI investigation of his role is toned down. He has also issued veiled threats to make public new details about the Irangate scandal, involving the release of US hostages which was allegedly delayed to benefit the Reagan/Bush presidential team. Adham's representatives in the US have told diplomats that relations between Washington and Saudi Arabia will be soured if the investigation is pursued. It may be no coincidence that the four regional investigations, at Tampa, Atlanta, Miami and Washington, have been reined in and brought under the direct control of the Department of Justice, a ministry which has been reluctant to pursue this case. However, Adham's star has now waned with the King of Saudi Arabia, and this looks an empty threat.

Hearings before the Senate sub-committee investigating BCCI, chaired by Senator John Kerry, have stoked up the controversy about security services involvement in the bank. He alleged in testimony that as early as 1981 US intelligence agents visited President Carter's budget director, Bert Lance, and British secret agents followed a year later. Lance said the agents were interested in finding out more about Irangate.

Suggestions that the Iran-Contra affair brought the then vice-president George Bush into at least indirect contact with BCCI have been strengthened following the release of documents in the United States. A British CIA agent, Leslie Alan Aspin, who has since died, claimed that he organised a BCCI-financed shipment of TOW missiles from Portugal to Iran on behalf of Oliver North in 1984. Aspin's statement and other personal documents released by his family are said to dovetail with North's own diaries which were only released in 1990, after Aspin's death. Officially, North was on the staff of the National Security Council in Washington at the time, but according to his diaries it is clear he was in frequent contact with the then vice-president. It is now being suggested in the US that North's reason for talking to Bush would have been to discuss arms deals and counter-terrorism.

The progress of the global investigations has not stopped efforts by some of the Gokals to return to business as usual. It appears that their Gulf Group, whose billions of dollars of loans were instrumental in bringing down the bank, is being rebuilt by a former employee of the three Gokal brothers, Zeyn Aly Mirza, from a safe haven in Tehran. Mirza, who worked for Euro Gulf, a subsidiary of Gulf, is setting up deals with German companies trading steel. Mirza denies working for a Gokal company, but is maintaining close links with ex-Gulf employees, notably Nigel Barrington, a former general manager of Gulf Steel, who now runs Britanico Trading in the United Kingdom.

Some members of the Gokal family are not having such an easy time. Mustafa Gokal is reported to be very upset and blaming BCCI for his company's problems. A member of the family living in Singapore has had to auction his house to cover debts, and Jiwad Gokal's house in Vancouver is under threat. The company's representative in Egypt had to flee the country by dead of night to escape house arrest.

In the United Kingdom a damage limitation exercise is in progress. The Sheikh of Abu Dhabi has hired a blue-blooded merchant bank, Schroders, to see whether a buyer could be found to keep some of the branches going as banks. They have also been told to dispose of the loan book. The British auditors Price Waterhouse, whose auditing performance was so heavily slated, continue to insist they were duped for fifteen years, and could not have exposed it earlier. They are waging a public relations campaign whose theme is that they cannot reveal the truth because of their duty of confidentiality. However, a British court has recently ruled that this duty would not be compromised if they gave their privileged account to the secret Bingham inquiry. A fly in the ointment is the revelation that PW itself borrowed money from BCCI in 1986. The firm's Barbados partnership took out a loan of $117,000 to refurbish their offices. The auditors' embarrassment does not give much comfort to Keith Vaz, who says he is devastated by the apparent hopelessness of the depositors' cause. The Labour MP is determined to keep on fighting to have the truth about the bank exposed.

The people who built the bank are not likely to help. Agha Hasan Abedi has returned to his home country and is now protected from the outside world by his wife, Rabia, at their compound in Karachi. He still suffers from the after-effects of his heart operations and can barely talk. In the few words he has uttered, it has become clear he is confessing nothing. He even made a bizarre suggestion that he should set up another bank to replace his last invention. While the ever-tolerant Pakistan authorities are prepared to allow Abedi to stay in Pakistan, and stifle attempts by the New York authorities to extradite him, setting up a bank would be too much even for them.

Another former senior executive of the bank, Ashraf

Nawabi, who headed up the Dubai operation and was very well connected with the al-Maktoum family, has reverted to the old BCCI stamping ground of Pakistani banking. Nawabi's application to set up a new bank in Pakistan had earlier been rejected because of his BCCI connections. But now, with the help of the al-Maktoums, he is thought to be bidding for 49 per cent of Abedi's old United Bank.

Ghassan Qassem, the bank manager turned MI5 informer who handled the Abu Nidal account in London, is leading a frightened existence, wary of all callers. Qassem has had to move his family out of his plush apartment in London's Maida Vale, and is now trying to get money out of MI5 for the legal costs he has incurred to clear his name from various smears carried in the press.

Manuel Noriega, the Panamanian dictator who banked with BCCI, is standing trial in Miami. He is threatening to make highly damaging accusations about George Bush's knowledge of Noriega's drug smuggling while he was head of the CIA in 1976. One player in Noriega's trial is Amjad Awan, his BCCI banker, who is thought to have bargained a remission in his sentence in return for co-operation with the US authorities.

Ali Reza Saheb, the man who knew Abedi when he was still dreaming of his world bank for Asians, is embittered and angry. Saheb treated Abedi as a man of honour, only to have his trust thrown back in his face. His life-savings lost, Saheb has retreated from the world of business and now studies the political prospects for his native Iran.

Robin Leigh-Pemberton, the Governor of the Bank of England, will have to wait for the publication of the Bingham report to know his future. A scathing indictment could, however, precipitate early retirement.

Robert Morgenthau and his men are criss-crossing the Atlantic, banging on doors of the authorities that once spurned them. Now they are greeted as heroes. They will continue to determine the direction of the BCCI story. The British Serious Fraud Office, which in any case had only the crumbs of the case to scoop up, has now had the embarrassment of seeing two of its investigators appear before Horseferry Road Magistrates Court, charged with the removal of confidential documents relating to BCCI. This happened immediately following a raid by the SFO on the offices of Control Securities and the homes of its chairman, Nazmu Virani, his brothers and BCCI manager Moizul Haque. Virani was named Asian businessman of the year last year and is currently in the top two hundred richest men in Britain. Virani's deals with Ghaith Pharaon to buy Spanish hotels may have been supported by BCCI money booked through BCCI (Overseas) in the Cayman Islands. The SFO is said to be currently investigating whether the deals were used to inflate BCCI's balance sheet.

At the December 2 hearing the winding up of the bank was postponed until January 14 1992. Touche Ross, the provisional liquidators, revealed that they had found assets of $1.159 billion and liabilities of $10.641 billion, making a likely yield for creditors of less than 10 per cent. Touche Ross also revealed the details of a pooled liquidation which will take effect in March 1992.

For many that will be a funeral for an unwanted relative; others will demand another autopsy, in a bid to ensure that the BCCI virus is not allowed to recur.

# BCCI in Numbers

The case against BCCI suggests many winners and many losers with figures running into billions of dollars. Listed below are just some of the names involved in the story with the amounts they are said to have handled. Not all broke the law. Sometimes the figures just point to one specific item on the balance-sheet as an example of the high stakes involved. They are not indicative of the full extent of the rewards; for example, Ziauddin Akbar is said to have received a $32 million bribe, which he denies, but he also received payments throughout an earlier term of imprisonment. Noriega is alleged to have plundered his country of hundreds of millions – he faces damages of more than $6 billion. Abedi handed out BCCI shares like confetti and they were later cashed in like coupons – precise figures may never be known.

Winners?

| | |
|---|---|
| Kamal Adham | $313 million |
| Ziauddin Akbar | $32 million |
| Robert Altman and Clark Clifford | $18 million |
| Faisal Saud al-Fulaij | $1 million |
| Alan Garcia | $50 million |
| Gokal brothers | $1.5 billion |
| Sheikh Humaid bin Rashid al-Naomi | $6.5 million |
| A. R. Khalil | $15 million |
| Khalid bin-Mahfouz | $528 million |

| | |
|---|---|
| Hector Neyra and Leonel Figueroa | $3 million |
| Ghaith Pharaon | $220 million |

Losers?

| | |
|---|---|
| UK depositors | Undisclosed millions |
| Spain and Gibraltar depositors | £83 million |
| Iranian depositors | $100 million |
| Western Isles Council | £23 million |
| Other councils | £30 million |
| Sheikh Zayed of Abu Dhabi | $5 billion |

BCCI Growth at a glance

| | |
|---|---|
| 1972 | Bank launched with $2.5 million capital base |
| 1973 | assets $20 million, capital $5.2 million, profits $335,000 |
| 1977 | assets $2.2 billion, capital $113 million, profits $26 million |
| 1984 | assets $16 billion |
| 1985 | assets $16.6 billion |
| 1986 | assets $17.5 billion |
| 1987 | assets $19.6 billion, profit $115.4 million |
| 1988 | first loss $49 million |
| 1989 | loss $498 million |

# Index